# FOOD & RECIPES

### OF THE SMOKIES

BY

Rose Houk

Great Smoky Mountains Association

© 1996 by Great Smoky Mountains Association

EDITED BY: Steve Kemp, Tom Robbins, & Glenn Cardwell
DESIGNED BY: Christina Watkins
TYPOGRAPHY & PRODUCTION BY: TypeWorks
ILLUSTRATED BY: Amy Campbell
COVER AND STILL LIFE PHOTOGRAPHS BY: Mary Ann Kressig
HISTORIC PHOTOGRAPHS COURTESY: National Park Service, Great Smoky
    Mountains National Park, and Douglas Redding (The Wolf Collection)
PROJECT COORDINATION BY: Steve Kemp
INVALUABLE ASSISTANCE BY: Jo Hoy, Alan and Jean Rock, and Coralie Bloom

Printed in the United States of America

7   8   9   10

ISBN 0-937207-22-5

WARNING: Do not eat any wild food without first positively identifying the plant. Follow safety instructions carefully when cooking with lye and when canning foods. The author and publisher of this book assume no liability for injuries which may occur to readers of this book who prepare foods described in this book.

GREAT SMOKY MOUNTAINS

Great Smoky Mountains Association is a private, nonprofit organization which supports the educational, scientific, and historical programs of Great Smoky Mountains National Park. Our publications are an educational service intended to enhance the public's understanding and enjoyment of the national park. If you would like to know more about our publications, memberships, guided hikes and other projects, please contact: Great Smoky Mountains Association, 115 Park Headquarters Road, Gatlinburg, TN 37738  (865) 436-7318 or visit www.SmokiesInformation.org.

# CONTENTS

# INTRODUCTION

> Ask any displaced Appalachian what he misses most about being away from the mountains and he will probably talk about soup beans, cornbread, sallet greens, fresh milk and butter, eggs, country ham, "and homemade biscuits every morning of the world."
> —Sidney Saylor Farr, *More Than Moonshine*

*On New Year's Day, to have plenty to eat all year, you must eat black-eyed peas and hog jowl, and every member of the family must stir the pot.*

Food in the Great Smoky Mountains was more than sustenance, it was, and still is, celebration. Every possible occasion—corn shuckin's, pea thrashin's, barn raisings, homecomings, and camp meetings, even the routine three meals a day—was reason for a feast.

Always on the table were the two staples of Smokies cuisine—pork and corn—prepared in an endless variety of ways. Rounding out the basic food groups were the constant accompaniments of beans, potatoes, pickles, and apples. And the desserts, my oh my. In this category, Smokies cooks showed their true talents. Berry pies, pumpkin pies, apple pies, puddings, and the highest state of the art—apple stack cakes—sweet enough to make a grown man weep.

The Cherokee Indians were the first to call the Great Smoky Mountains home. They had lived in the southern Appalachians for more than a thousand years before Europeans arrived on the scene. After the Revolutionary War, the European settlers moved westward into the Smokies and laid claim to the rich river bottomlands of these mountains that span the border between North Carolina and Tennessee. The newcomers found the Cherokees already growing their own variety of flour corn. The European farmers, mostly Scotch-Irish, English and German, would widely adopt a strain called Hickory Cane or Hickory King, which became commercially available in the mid 1800s. It's white, not yellow corn, as any self-respecting mountain farmer will quickly note. Yankees grow yellow corn.

Nearly everything mountain people ate—both animal and vegetable—was by necessity gathered or raised by their own hands. In the words of Beuna Winchester, of Bryson City, North

Carolina, it was this simple: "You ate what you raised and you raised what you ate."

In spring, a Smokies farmer began the yearly round of clearing, plowing, and planting his cornfield, while women put in cool-weather crops in their big gardens, and herbs by the garden gate. They carefully selected and saved seeds and grew a host of vegetables and fruits, many now considered precious heirlooms. Crops flourished in the warm, rainy summer months. In late summer a bounty of garden produce set off a frenzy of preserving, and after the mid 1800s, canning too. When the weather turned cool in October and the leaves on the trees shaded into colors of stained glass, it was time to make sorghum molasses. A month or more later, once it was thoroughly cold, the corn was picked and stored and hogs and a few steers were butchered.

**Ploughing with an ox.**
*circa 1938 by H. C. Wilburn*

A typical summer day for a Smokies family often started with a hearty breakfast of eggs, biscuits, gravy, and sausage, though sometimes a person had only cornmeal mush with milk. Then, the whole family walked to the fields. Before noon, women headed home to fix "dinner," the main meal of the day, consisting of hot cornbread, beans, pork in some form, and possibly a dessert. Duly fortified, they went back out to the cornfield for the afternoon. What appeared on the table for supper often closely resembled what was left over from dinner.

In addition to what they grew, Smokies mountaineers learned quickly that these old, forested mountains spilled forth a cornucopia of wild foods: greens, berries, nuts, game and fish.

The rhythms of peoples' lives were inextricably tied to the rhythms of the seasons and nature's bounty—fresh cress in early spring, juicy blackberries in summer, savory walnuts in the fall.

Preserving the harvest was crucial, for there were no refrigerators and no supermarkets in the Smoky Mountains. Pork was cured with salt and hung in the smokehouse. Milk and butter were kept cool down at the springhouse. Beans were strung and dried and hung in the attic. Barrels of beans and corn pickled in a salty brine were kept in a cool corner of the cabin or in the meathouse. Apples, dried and sulphured, were kept by the barrelfuls too. Potatoes and other root crops were buried in the ground. The Mason jar was patented in 1858, and once these glass "cans," or jars, became available in the mountains, women put up gallons upon gallons of fruits and vegetables and lined them up in neat rows in the "can house" or cellar. Nearly every farmstead had a corncrib of functional design, and a few had apple houses.

*Cooking for a big family was no small chore. The Jonathan Tipton family lived in Cades Cove where Mr. Tipton operated the Cable Mill for a time. circa 1930 courtesy Randolph Shields*

In the deep hollows between the high peaks of the Great Smokies, some families lived in isolation. For them, it was a long walk or horseride to commune with their neighbors, go to the community store, or take corn to the mill. But mountain folk were sturdy walkers and would travel far out of their way for those things they couldn't supply for themselves.

Horace Kephart, a midwestern librarian who settled in the wilds of Deep Creek in the early 1900s, told of Long Goody, a woman who stood six feet, three inches tall. She "walked eighteen miles across the Smokies into Tennessee, crossing at an elevation of 5,000 feet, merely to shop more advantageously than she could at home. The next day she shouldered fifty pounds of flour and some other groceries, and bore them home before nightfall." At the store, people traded or sold eggs from their chickens and honey from their bees for coffee, salt, sugar, baking soda, baking powder, and a few exotic spices.

As for rural people everywhere, self sufficiency for southern mountaineers was a necessity, but no less so than the willingness of every person to help his neighbor if he could. A Smokies visitor never left a home hungry, no matter how little the family had in the cupboard. Food was not a measure of wealth, for everyone ate mostly the same things—common, filling, honest food without pretensions.

Names of places in the Smokies evoke thoughts of food and times when rations were scarce: Poor Fork, Poverty, No Pone, Burnt Pone, No Fat, Needmore, Long Hungry, Raw Dough, Sandy Mush, Sugar Fork, Ramp Cove, Meat-scaffold Branch, Fodder-stack, and more than one Mill Creek.

The earliest cooking was done over a campfire along the trail. As cabins with fireplaces were built, the campfire was simply moved indoors. Food was boiled, fried, and baked in iron kettles and pots over the fire and in ashes on the hearth. When a little cash came a family's way, they might invest in a Home Comfort or Blue Ridge wood cookstove, which admirably served double duty both for cooking and warming the house. Woodstoves brought another great advance. Instead of constantly stooping to stir the pots at the fireplace, a cook could stand up straight.

Woodstove cookery was an artform in itself: starting a fire in the firebox, keeping the biscuits from burning in the oven while hefting cast iron pans and skillets from one stove eye (or burner) to another. Woodstoves had the added features of a warming oven where a pan of biscuits could be set aside, and a holding tank on the side filled with water ready for dishwashing.

How did a person learn to cook? If a cook did refer to a book, it was most likely the *Home Comfort Cookbook of Home Cooking and Canning,* put out by the Wrought Iron Range Company in Saint Louis, or the *Rumford Complete Cook Book,* published at the turn of the century by the Rumford Baking Powder Company. For the most part, though, mountain cooking was oral tradition. A youngster learned the basics through the tutoring of Granny or Mama, who passed along the wisdom of how to pluck a chicken, chop sauerkraut, sulphur apples, and bake a perfect biscuit. Measurements and proportions were rarely specific. "All good cooks," declared Lucinda Ogle of Gatlinburg, "go by pinches and dabs."

**Louisa Walker hoes at the Walker Sisters' farm in Little Greenbrier.** *1936 by E. E. Exline*

Without doubt, cooking three stout meals a day for a family of twelve was at times a chore, but a chore often performed with pleasure and pride. As Glenn Cardwell, of Greenbrier, Tennessee, remembered: "On Sunday my mother never knew whether to cook for ten or for twenty . . . but she did it with joy."

In the old days, chicken didn't come in boxes, biscuits didn't come in cans, and bacon didn't come in plastic. There were no mixes, microwave ovens, or food processors, and no such thing as fast food. On the hearth of a fireplace, a pone of cornbread baked slowly to a golden brown. On the back burner of a stove, a pot of beans bubbled for several hours. In the smokehouse, a ham hung for a year.

Were those former days really better? Beuna Winchester believes so: "They said it was the good old days, and it really was because it was so much more peaceful then." Part of that peace involved sitting on the front porch of an evening snapping fresh green beans, inhaling the irresistible scents of food cooking on a woodstove, saying grace over a meal served to family and friends, and knowing the comfort that good, simple mountain food can bring.

## A NOTE ABOUT THE RECIPES

The aim of this book is to feature the foods and recipes common and popular in the Great Smoky Mountains before the national park was created in 1934. It covers the time from the Cherokee Indians, through the nineteenth and into the mid twentieth centuries.

To create the park all the private parcels of land were purchased, and residents eventually had to move away. Yet, many people stayed near the Smokies, held by ties to family and love of the place. They seemed to adhere to the belief among mountain people that you should never go so far away you can't see the smoke from your parents' chimney. Many of them, and their descendants, still hunt, gather, eat, and cook the way their foremothers and forefathers did, albeit with more modern methods and utensils. They must do their hunting and gathering outside the park now.

While almost all the recipes are adaptable to modern electric and gas stoves, they are still "made from scratch" as they were prepared in pre-park days. Bowing to the interests of modern health concerns, one major ingredient has in most cases been changed. Lard rendered from hogs was the solid shortening used by nearly all mountain cooks in the old days. Many of the recipes now call for vegetable shortening instead. We do not suggest substituting liquid shortening, because it will alter the consistency of the food.

We have made every effort to give credit to the person who supplied a recipe, or to the book from which it came. But one of the beauties of recipes is that they are handed down from one generation to the next and passed from friend to friend; their true origin has often been lost along the way.

**Drying beans and fruit in the Davis/ Queen house at the Oconaluftee Mountain Farm Museum.** *by Mary Ann Kressig*

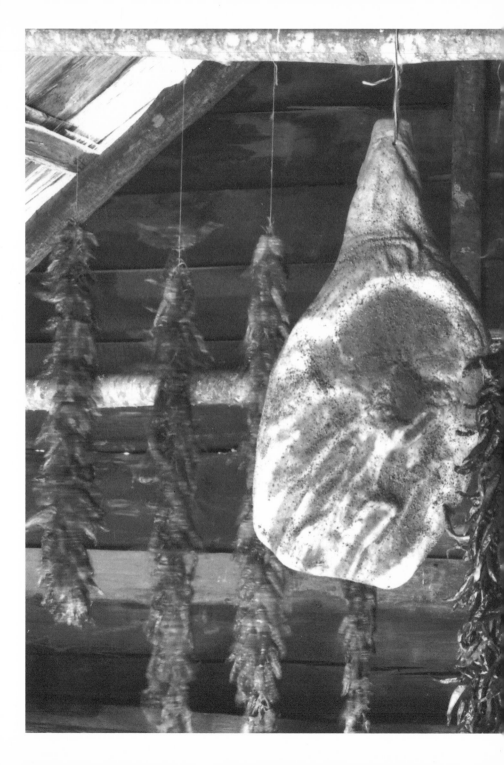

# MEATS &
# MAIN DISHES

### O F   T H E   S M O K I E S

# MEATS & MAIN DISHES

"I can't remember a meal put down on the table that didn't have
meat with it. Had to have meat and bread. . . two things we were
never without."                                    —Beuna Winchester

In the Smoky Mountains, the words "meat" and "pork"
were synonymous. To most people, meat meant fried ham,
bacon, sausage, and backbones and ribs. Beans and greens were
not properly cooked without a chunk of fatback, or salt pork,
laid in with them. Even the head of a pig, "rooter" and all, was
cooked into something called souse, or head cheese. The
drippings in the pan never went to waste either. They were put
to proper use in red-eye or sawmill gravy, essential for sopping
biscuits.

"The mainstay of every farmer, aside from his cornfield, was
his litter of razorback hogs," observed Horace Kephart. And "in
the mountains it is more heinous to kill another man's pig than
to shoot the owner." To show ownership, the hogs' ears were
clipped with distinctive marks or pierced with a brass ring.

Pork was the meat of choice in the early days because it was
easier to preserve than beef and did not require refrigeration.
Also, hog husbandry didn't require as much effort. Most of the
year hogs were simply left to run in the woods, eating their fill of
frogs, snakes, roots, bulbs, acorns, and chestnuts, at least before
the chestnut blight completely wiped out the species.

Some mountaineers took their hogs up to the grassy balds
and let them graze. These high mountain meadows, such as
Gregory Bald and Spence Field above Cades Cove, may have
actually maintained their open character by virtue of animal
grazing. Roy Myers of Tuckaleechee Cove recalled, "Them hogs
stayed up there all winter, part of 'em," and when it snowed
people carried corn up to them. Often, the hogs were brought
down for the last few weeks before butchering, put in a pen, and
fattened on corn; this final fattening was thought to produce
better lard.

On a cold, frosty morning around Thanksgiving, it was

time to butcher. Some mountaineers insisted this should take place when the moon was waxing, for if pigs were killed in the waning moon the meat would shrink or spoil. Hubert Sullivan, whose great-grandfather Daniel Ledbetter helped build the Cable Mill in Cades Cove, said they always liked to kill hogs on the old moon, just past full.

Three or four hogs might be slaughtered at one time, and it helped to have a few extra hands from surrounding farms join in. First, a big fire was built. Then water was boiled in a big iron wash kettle, and the dead pig was dipped in to scald off the hairs. Alternatively, the hog was hung by the hind legs and boiling water was poured over it. With a butcher knife, the hair was scraped off, the hog was gutted, and then the meat was trimmed up into hams, shoulders, loins, backbones and ribs, and bacon and fatback (also called middlings or "streaked meat").

Earl, Horace, Collie, and Willard Ogle butcher a hog in the "Glades" near Gatlinburg.

Pork was preserved several ways. A dry salt cure (sometimes with sugar added) was patted onto the hams. This was done only after the animal's body heat had dissipated. If the meat was salted when still "hot" (with the animal's body heat), it would turn out too salty to eat. In the meathouse, bacon and fatback were laid on shelves, and shoulders of ham were suspended from the rafters.

Some people simply hung a "green ham" and let it cure, while others smoked it in a smokehouse to add flavor and protect the meat from insects. Hickory was the favorite wood for smoking. A whole book could be written on the art of smoking hams. Beuna Winchester described one method followed in her part of the country: Build a fire in an old wash pot, let it smolder, and put red pepper on the embers. Hold your breath when you go in, and don't stay in long. Start the fire "early of a morning," let it smolder all day, then let it go out at night. Do this for four or five days, for a total smoking time of thirty-six to forty-eight hours. "When it [the meat] takes what smoke it's going to take, that's all it's going to take," Beuna said.

The meat was "wropped" in brown paper and put in cloth seed and flour sacks. Some people believed the ham should be left to "sweat" through the summer months. Pieces of it were sliced off as needed and salt rubbed into the cut spot. "That was country ham, the real country ham," declared Beuna. How long the genuine article should age remains a matter of intent discussion among those who love this form of pork. A ham can hang for only six or eight weeks and be ready to eat. It can even be cured for up to a year, but few would let it go more than two years. The meat was supposed to get moldy and crusty looking and covered with white specks on the outside. If a ham was overly salty, a piece could be soaked in buttermilk for a day to make it more edible.

Backbones and ribs were eaten fresh, while sausage was fried, put in jars or crocks, and covered with lard to preserve it. Some people stored the unfried sausage in cornhusks and hung them from the smokehouse rafters. Fat was saved from the skin and entrails of the hog, cut into pieces about the size of a hen's egg, and cooked in a big black kettle, slowly so it wouldn't scorch or "swivvle up." The white, fluffy "leaf lard" from the entrails was considered the best for biscuits. Lard was so important in Southern cooking that the author of a book published in 1860 termed it "the very oil that moves the machinery of life." Even the brown residue left in the bottom of the pot after lard-making, called cracklings, was incorporated into a cornbread called "cracklin' bread."

In the 1920s and 1930s, the almost universal reliance on pork products was broken, but only a little, by the coming of company stores to logging camps in the Smokies. Here, people could purchase imported foods such as bologna sausage. Dorie Cope, who lived and cooked in the camps, said this meat was a "rare treat. . . . It tasted like manna from heaven after a steady diet of ham, bacon, salt pork, dried pork, boiled pork, and fried pork."

Second only to pork in the meat department was chicken. Nearly everyone raised chickens, so many they didn't bother preserving them but always ate them fresh. Excess roosters were fated to become fryers. It was as simple as going out into the barnyard, catching the chicken, wringing its neck, defeathering, singeing the hairs off, then cutting the bird into quarters for frying. Broiler-sized chickens were boiled and used in that hearty, rib-sticking main dish, chicken and dumplings. Chicken was Sunday fare, fed to the preacher when he visited for revivals or church services. Mountain folk joked that young boys who especially liked chicken were being prepared by God to preach. Like many other staunchly religious mountain people, Dorie Cope and her family enjoyed "all-day singing and dinner on the grounds" at church on Sundays. "We'd get up early, kill and fry a chicken, take Saturday's cake, and have a good time," said Dorie.

Chickens had the added benefit of supplying eggs used in cooking or as items for sale or barter. Throughout the Smokies, an institution known as the "rolling store" developed after the

*My old hen,
she clucks
a lot.
Next time she
clucks, she's
cluckin' in
the pot.*

*My old hen,
she clucks
a lot.
Next time she
clucks, she's
cluckin' in
the pot.*

**Peddler with dressed chicken.** *circa 1926–29 by Laura Thornborough*

community stores had closed in the 1920s and 1930s. A mobile merchant, complete with chicken coop atop his vehicle, made the rounds once every week or two, dispensing special delicacies such as coconut and candy in return for local eggs, butter, and vegetables.

Cattle and sheep were raised in the Smokies too, but not as commonly as pigs or chickens. If a family had cattle, they would butcher one and divide the beef among kinfolk and neighbors. Roy Myers and his father grazed a large herd of cattle on Defeat

*Joel Proctor and Earnest, Floyd, and Luther Abbot with trout.*
*courtesy Randolph Shields*

Ridge. Each animal had a bell around its neck. Cattle were put onto the balds in the spring and left to graze among the hills and hollers. In autumn, they were rounded up and driven to markets in Knoxville and other towns; Roy Myers got three cents a pound for steers. Durhams, white-faced, and Angus were common breeds raised in the region.

Fish were a big part of many peoples' diets because they were so abundant in the thousand miles of swift, clear streams and rivers that flow down the Smoky Mountains. Beuna Winchester said her brothers just walked down the holler and set up a fish trap at the mouth of the branch. They caught catfish, and anything not needed for the table was released back into the stream. When they went camping, they set a trot line across river, baited hooks, and caught blue cats and channel cats. Beuna said her Mama would fillet fish with a good sharp knife, roll them in cornmeal, and fry them in hot grease "in a heartbeat."

In March and April, fish called stonerollers were among the delectables found on mountain tables. People also fished for brook trout, the one local people called "spec," a species once common but now found only in the highest reaches of streams. On the Tennessee side of the Smokies, Lucinda Ogle recollected fishing for brook trout in Le Conte Creek nearly all year long. In the side pools of the creek they gathered "stick bait," caddisfly larvae that build cases of sticks and pebbles around themselves. Fishing poles were made of river cane, collected in autumn when the cane was dry. "I believe God put the fish in that creek for us," said Lucinda.

John Stinnett with his rifle, powder horn, and pouch.
*courtesy Elsie Burrell*

The woods and streams were filled with edible game: rabbit, squirrel, groundhog, opossum, raccoon, wild turkey, turtle, frog, deer, bear, grouse, and dove. The Cherokees dined on yellowjacket soup and fried locusts, foods the European settlers never seemed to take to with great enthusiasm.

When snow covered the ground, rabbits could be tracked to brush piles. Around Thanksgiving rabbits were especially popular because they were fat and good to hunt at that time of year. Rabbit was usually baked or fried.

Unlike rabbit, squirrel was often made into a stew. Beuna Winchester's mother boiled squirrel and made a white gravy with it, best accompanied by hot biscuits. Early in the fall, Hubert Sullivan said he "still hunted" squirrels, that is he went into the woods without his dogs, while the leaves were still on the trees and the squirrels were "working on hickory nuts." As

**Arthur and Bill Moore with gun, ax, hound, and the rewards of a successful squirrel hunt.**

winter arrived and the trees dropped their leaves, Hubert hunted squirrels with his dog. He went after squirrels in the daytime and raccoons at night.

Most mountain people ate groundhog and opossum only out of desperation. Common instructions for preparing 'possum were to parboil, bake, and put on a board. Then throw away the 'possum and eat the board.

By all reports, wild turkeys were once more plentiful in the mountains and there for the taking, as they fed on chestnuts and beechnuts. Deer, on the other hand, were not as abundant historically as they are today in the park. Black bears were hunted for the meat, and those who hunted them became legends in their own time, men like Old Black Bill Walker, herder Tom Sparks, and "Turkey" George Palmer of Cataloochee. Black bears were taken for their hides and tallow as well. Bear steak and venison jerky certainly filled empty stomachs at times.

Meat was one food few mountain people went without. As an indication of how highly it was regarded, if meat was lacking the meal was simply called "poor do."

**Killing a Wild Turkey required considerable skill.** *by Richard P. Smith*

## Country Ham & Red-eye Gravy

Bruce Whaley,
Gatlinburg, TN,
*Gatlinburg Recipe
Collection*

Slice of country ham
(about ¹/₃-inch thick)

1 tsp corn oil
Water or black coffee (for gravy)

Trim off outside skin from ham, leaving some of the fat. Put corn oil in an iron skillet, enough to grease bottom of pan. Heat skillet and fry ham until slightly brown on both sides. (Ham doesn't take long to cook). Remove ham to warm platter and make red-eye gravy by adding ¹/₄ to ¹/₂ cup of water to hot skillet, let sizzle, and pour over ham. (Add a small amount of black coffee, if desired).

"Biscuits always go well with country ham, and when I was a kid I liked to sop my biscuits in red-eye gravy. I am not a kid anymore but I still like to sop a biscuit in red-eye gravy. I also like to grill country ham on a charcoal or gas grill."

## Sugar Cure

Enough for one ham or one shoulder.

1 pint salt
4 Tbsp brown sugar

2 Tbsp black pepper
1 tsp red pepper

Cover ham with mixture, wrap in brown paper and tie firmly, put in cloth sack (a clean sheet of unbleached muslin, domestic cotton) and hang in safe, cool place for about six weeks. Always hang meat with shank end down.

## Another version of Sugar Cure

Louise Woodruff,
Walland, TN

Makes enough for 200 pounds of pork (whole ham, shoulder, or side meat).

1 c. salt
1 Tbsp white sugar

1 tsp saltpeter
1 Tbsp black pepper

Mix ingredients well, then rub skin side of meat real hard, then rub other side. Wrap in paper a little, not too tight. Put in cloth bag with shank down. When dripping stops, take out and hang upright. Let cure 5–6 weeks before cooking, or longer.

One ham        Cloves

Brown sugar      Apple cider

## Baked Ham

Ferne Shelton, Southern Appalachian Mountain Cookbook

Wash ham thoroughly and place in large kettle. Cover with water and cook slowly until tender, 20–30 minutes per pound of meat. Remove from kettle and remove outside skin. With a knife, score the surface of ham; sprinkle with brown sugar and dot with cloves. Bake about 45 minutes at 350 degrees, basting with cider.

---

Pork backbones and ribs      Salt and pepper

Water

## Backbones & Ribs

Sidney Saylor Farr, More Than Moonshine

From butchered hog, chop fresh backbones and ribs into serving pieces and put in heavy kettle. Add water to cover and salt and pepper to taste. Cook until meat is tender.

Fresh backbones and ribs are delicious with cornbread, cooked turnips and greens, and other vegetables. They are also good served with biscuits or hot rolls, with the broth spooned over the bread.

To can, brown pieces in oven for about 30 minutes, pack in hot jars, add 1 teaspoon salt to each quart, cover with boiling water. Seal jars and process in pressure cooker, for amount of time specified in current canning instructions.

---

Pork chops        Salt and pepper

Flour            Lard and butter

## Fried Pork Chops (Mountain Style)

Ferne Shelton, Southern Appalachian Mountain Cookbook

Season chops with salt and pepper. Roll in flour. Fry in hot lard and butter until brown on both sides. Reduce heat to low, and cook until tender.

## Old-Fashioned Souse

Sidney Saylor Farr, *More Than Moonshine*

Souse, sometimes called head cheese or scrapple, is made of the cleaned head of a butchered hog.

| | |
|---|---|
| *6 c. chopped meat* | *2 tsp red pepper* |
| *1 quart broth* | *1 1/2 tsp allspice* |
| *3 tsp salt* | *2 tsp cloves* |
| *4 tsp black pepper* | |

Clean hog's head by removing snout, eyes, ears, brains, and all the skin and fat. Cut the head into four pieces and soak in salt water (1/2 cup salt to 1 gallon water) for 3 to 5 hours to draw out all the blood. Drain and wash pieces in clear water. Cover meat with hot water and boil until meat separates from the bones.

Remove meat and chop well. Strain the broth, adding water if needed to make a quart of liquid. Mix the salt, black and red pepper, allspice, and cloves into the broth. Then drop in the chopped meat, mix thoroughly, and put in a loaf pan or other container with straight sides to set. Keep in a cool place. Slice and use as needed. Can be served with cooked dried beans, cornbread, and vegetables.

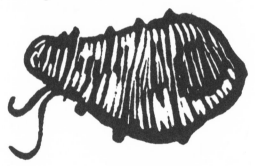

## Pork Sausage

Sidney Saylor Farr, *More Than Moonshine*

| *Pork* | *Pepper* |
|---|---|
| *Salt* | *Hot pepper (to taste)* |

Select pieces of meat to be used for sausage and cut into small pieces. To each gallon of meat, add 2 rounded tablespoons of salt and 1 rounded tablespoon of pepper. Mix thoroughly and put through meat grinder. When meat is all ground, it is ready for use. Make into patties, and cook fresh. To preserve, cook patties and pack in jars with lard over them. Store in cool place.

*Sliced pork loin*
*Flour*

*Milk*
*Salt and pepper*

## Pork Loin & Gravy

Mrs. Ollie Lawhern, Maryville-Alcoa Times

Slice pork loin in $1/4$- to $1/2$-inch-thick slices. Dip in flour and coat until white. Heat pork grease in iron skillet. When hot, drop in meat, brown on both sides. When browned, cover with lid and cook slowly until tender and juicy. Remove meat to platter, add two "rounding" spoons of flour to cooking juice, mix in thoroughly, add milk, salt and pepper to taste, and cook slowly, stirring until gravy is smooth.

---

*$3/4$ tsp salt, divided*
*$1/2$ tsp pepper, divided*
*$2^1/2$ lbs. pork loin end roast*
*$1/2$ c. flour*
*$1/4$ c. melted butter*

*2 Tbsp oil*
*1 medium onion, chopped*
*4 carrots, cut in short pieces*
*4 medium potatoes, peeled &*
  *halved*

## Southern Pork Roast

Duane Oliver, Cooking on Hazel Creek

Rub $1/2$ tsp salt and $1/4$ tsp pepper over roast, dredge roast in flour. Brown on all sides in butter and oil in deep, large cast iron skillet. Remove roast from skillet, drain. Sauté onion in pan drippings until tender. Place roast over onions, add carrots and potatoes. Sprinkle remaining salt and pepper over vegetables. Cover and bake at 350 degrees for $1^1/2$ hours. Transfer roast to serving platter. Drain vegetables and place around roast. Slice and serve.

---

*Liver of hog (or beef)*
*Grease*

*Flour*
*Onions*

## Liver & Onions

Glenn Cardwell, Greenbrier, TN

The fresh liver of a hog (or beef) was a feast often eaten on the second day after butchering. To prepare, slice liver into $1/4$-inch thick slices and roll in flour (use some salt if desired). In a greased iron skillet, brown liver slices on each side. After turning, add the chopped onions, cook until transparent, and serve over top of cooked liver.

## Hog Jowls & Peas

Glenn Cardwell,
Greenbrier, TN

This traditional dish was eaten on New Year's Day to bring good luck. In some parts of the South, this dish is commonly served with rice, and is called Hoppin' John.

*1 lb. dried peas*        *Hog jowl*
*(black-eyed, cornfield,*
  *or clay peas)*

Soak peas overnight, drain, add fresh water and simmer about two hours, or until peas are done. Season with salt and pepper to taste. Fry hog jowl and serve alongside peas. Fried potatoes, late turnip greens or sauerkraut, cornbread, and pickles and relishes rounded out the menu.

---

## Chicken & Dumplings

Mrs. Ollie
Lawhern,
Maryville-Alcoa
Times

*One hen*        *Salt and pepper*

Catch an old hen that is contrary about laying. Chop off her head, dress her, cut her up, and place her in a pot. Just cover her with water and place her on to simmer. When tender, season with salt and pepper to taste. You can leave her with the meat on the bones or take the meat off. Into the boiling pot liquor, drop dumpling dough a spoonful at a time.

**DUMPLING DOUGH**

*2 c. flour*        *3 Tbsp lard or vegetable*
*3 Tbsp baking powder*      *shortening*
*1 tsp salt*        *1 well-beaten egg*
             *1 c. whole milk*

Sift together flour, baking powder, and salt. Cut in lard or shortening and mix in egg and milk. Drop into pot liquor that cooked chicken in. Cover and cook for 15 minutes.

---

## Chicken

"If the preacher was coming, she'd cook two chickens so there would be plenty of meat in the broth."

Wring a chicken's neck, pluck feathers, cut into quarters, roll in flour, and fry in grease just a few minutes. After chickens get to broiler size, that's when we'd have boiled chicken, for chicken and dumplings. Mama always took the chicken off the bone.

Beuna Winchester, Bryson City, NC

## DUMPLINGS

"Mama put black pepper on top of dumplings before she put the lid on. She did that so she could tell if we'd been in to them."

*Flour*                    *Lard*

Fat is where you get the flavor for dumplings. Make dumplings about like biscuits, but use less grease because it makes them light and fluffy rather than "heavy and packy." Eliminate excess fat and skin from chicken and use lean meat, take all the bones out, get liquid to rolling boil, then pinch off tiny balls of dough and drop one at a time into the chicken broth. Set pot back on cooler part of stove, put lid on and keep on until get ready to serve. (Dumplings look just like biscuits but are not brown.)

---

In the old days, mountain folk had flocks of chickens. Eggs, stewed chicken with dumplings, and fried chicken were mainstays of the diet. Early spring would bring the clucking of hens. They were "set" with 12 to 15 eggs, carefully selected. In twenty-one days, the new chicks began hatching. In about 12 weeks, the roosters ended up on the dinner table. The pullets were kept to add to the flock as egg producers.

Fried Chicken

Bonnie Myers, Townsend, TN

*Young fryer,*           *Grease*
*about two pounds*       *Salted flour*

Slaughter chicken by wringing and breaking neck. Hold chicken upside down by the legs and pour scalding water over it. Pluck feathers. Hold chicken over a burning newspaper to singe thin growth of hairy feathers. Cut up chicken. Roll in salted flour and place in hot grease in heavy fryer pan. Fry slowly, turning once or twice to brown evenly.

## Chicken & Corn

### Tsi-Ta-Ga A-Su-Yi Se-Lu

Mrs. Clifford
Hornbuckle,
Cherokee NC,
*Cherokee Cooklore*

One chicken

Skinned corn

Salt and pepper

Stew chicken until well done, then add cooked, skinned corn (as for hominy). Cook together long enough to get a good flavor. Beans may be added if desired. Season to taste with salt and pepper.

---

## Fish & Hushpuppies

Beuna Winchester,
Bryson City, NC

"Fish start off when it's soft and is done when it's firm."

Fish fillets

Cornmeal

Roll fish fillets in cornmeal and drop in hot grease, turn one time. Make hush puppies out of cornmeal and fry in the same grease you fried the fish in. Drain fish on a brown paper bag, and set on the lid of the stove closet to keep good and hot.

### HUSHPUPPIES

1 c. self-rising white
  cornmeal
$1/2$ c. self-rising white flour
$1/2$ tsp salt
1 tsp sugar

1 egg (blended in)
Buttermilk (enough to produce
  this batter, up to 1 c.)
Pepper to taste
Chopped onion, if desired

Combine all ingredients into thick batter and roll into balls. Fry in grease.

---

## Fish & Mush

Mrs. Katie Taylor
Brady,
Cherokee, NC,
*Cherokee Cooklore*

Fish

Water

Cornmeal

Soda

Barbecue fish by cooking on a stick, then cut into small pieces and boil in water to make a thick soup. Make mush by cooking cornmeal with a little lye or soda and water. Eat the mush with the fish soup. This dish was always served to sick people when fish were available.

"Mama cooked a lot of rabbit, just the little old wild brown rabbits that hopped around in the woods."

**Rabbit**

Beuna Winchester,
Bryson City, NC

Bake a rabbit, or if you have a mature, older rabbit, simmer until almost tender and then bake. Rabbit was supposed to be eaten as dry meat; never saw her make a rabbit stew.

---

"She [Mama] has cooked a groundhog . . . but at the time you could get groundhog you was kind of hungry for meat, probably."

**Country Groundhog**

Beuna Winchester,
Bryson City, NC

*1 young groundhog*
*1¹/4 c. flour*
*¹/4 tsp baking soda*
*¹/4 tsp salt*

*Pepper*
*1 Tbsp sugar*
*1¹/4 c. warm water*

Soak the groundhog in salt water overnight. Cut meat into serving pieces. Combine flour, baking soda, salt, and pepper and rub onto meat. Brown in hot fat, then sprinkle with sugar. Add water, and simmer covered 40 minutes.

Another version of cooking groundhog that would help get rid of the wild flavor: Parboil with hot pepper and onion, 45 minutes to an hour, shift to fresh clean water, then add another pepper and onion and cook until tender. Bake as with rabbit.

*One squirrel*
*Flour*

*Milk*

**Squirrel Stew**

Beuna Winchester,
Bryson City, NC

Boil the squirrel and make a white gravy on it. Pour the gravy into the broth the squirrel was cooked in.

## Squirrel Dumplings

Bonnie Myers, Townsend, TN

| One squirrel | Water |
| Salt | |

In the mountains, squirrels fattened on American chestnuts. Squirrels were hunted in the fall. A hunter brought his kill home, then skinned, gutted, and cleaned it. The head and limbs were separated, and the body was washed in cold, salted water. To cook a squirrel, put it into a gallon-size heavy pot. Add salt and enough water to cover. Boil gently until tender. While this simmers, add dumplings, one by one.

### DUMPLINGS

| 2 c. all-purpose flour | $^1/_2$ c. butter |
| 1 tsp salt | Milk |

Cut butter into flour-salt mixture and add enough milk to work into soft dough. Turn out onto floured board. Add flour to roll out, and roll thin. Cut into one-inch squares.

---

## Opossum

Lucinda Ogle, Gatlinburg, TN

| Opossum | Sweet potatoes |
| Spicebush | |

Some mountain people would not eat opossum because they did not believe they were "clean" animals. But Lucinda Ogle, who grew up on Scratch Britches Creek beneath Mount Le Conte in the Smokies, tells how her Grandpappy Oakley made opossum "so anybody could eat it."

First he boiled the 'possum to get the grease out of it. While it was boiling, he'd say, "Lucinda child, run out there and get me a bundle of spicebushes." She'd bring a little bundle of them back, and he would boil the spicebush with the 'possum to take out any wild taste. Then he'd brown the meat and bake in the oven of the woodstove with sweet potatoes around it.

*Meat skins, any kind*     *Cornmeal*
*Salt*

**Meat Skin Soup**

Boil meat skins until they are done, then bake or roast until brown. Put in water with a little salt and boil until it has good flavor. Thicken with cornmeal and cook until the meal is done.

William Crowe and Goingback Chiltoskey, Cherokee, NC, *Cherokee Cooklore*

---

Catch crayfish by baiting them with groundhog meat or buttermilk. Pinch off the tails and legs and discard the rest. Parboil, remove the hulls and fry the little meat that is left. When crisp, it is ready to eat. May also be made into soup or stew after being fried.

**Crayfish**

Mrs. Clifford Hornbuckle, *Cherokee Cooklore*

---

Catch early frogs, called knee-deeps, scald and skin. Parboil and cook like other meats.

**Knee-Deeps** *Du-S-Du*

Aggie Ross Lossiah, *Cherokee Cooklore*

---

*Frog legs*          *Salt and pepper to taste*
*2 eggs*             *Cracker crumbs or flour*
*1 c. milk*          *Lard or oil*

**Fried Frog Legs**

Boil frog legs in salt water for 3 minutes; drain. Beat eggs in milk, add salt and pepper, and mix well. Dip each frog leg in egg and milk mixture, then in cracker crumbs or flour. Fry in heavy skillet in very hot lard or cooking oil. Fry until rich brown and serve at once.

Sidney Saylor Farr, *More Than Moonshine*

---

These large turtles are found in summer along many mountain streams, often at lower elevations. To catch a snapping turtle, grab it by the tail. According to Glenn, if you get bit by one "it won't turn a body loose until the sun goes down."

**Snapping Turtle**

Glenn Cardwell, Greenbrier, TN

One snapping turtle          Grease
Flour

Catch turtle, cut off head, remove intestines, and cut body into frying-sized pieces. Roll pieces in flour with salt and pepper, fry in grease as would chicken. All of it was white meat, though in the same turtle some of the meat would taste like fish, other parts like chicken. One large turtle fed nine people at the Cardwell table.

---

## Beef Steak & Gravy

Bonnie Myers,
Townsend, TN

Early-day beef slaughter usually took place during cold weather. Neighbors were proud recipients, as there were few means of preserving that amount of meat.

Beef steak          2 c. milk
Salt                1 c. water
Flour

Pound beef steak with wooden mallet, salt and roll in flour, then place in heavy cooker, along with fat, and brown. Add about two more tablespoons of flour, plus the milk and water. Stir until gravy is thickened.

---

## Pot Roast of Beef

Bea and Paul
Cable, in Duane
Oliver's
*Cooking on Hazel
Creek*

4 lbs. top sirloin of beef        Onions
3 level Tbsp meat drippings       Carrots
1 qt. boiling water               Turnips
2 level Tbsp flour

Have the meat cut in a thick, compact piece. If necessary, tie and skewer so it will keep its shape. Melt drippings in a saucepan (an old-fashioned, round-bottom Scotch Bowl is best), and brown meat on all sides. Pour the boiling water over the meat and cover closely. Simmer gently for 2 hours. Season and add chopped vegetables. Cook until vegetables are tender, then remove meat and vegetables from pan and thicken gravy with the flour mixed smoothly with a little cold water. If necessary, add more water while the roast is cooking, so there will be enough gravy to cover the vegetables.

---

Meatloaf was (and still is) a standard dish at church socials and meetings, as well as homecoming and reunion potluck dinners.

### Meatloaf

Faye Cardwell,
Greenbrier, TN

| | |
|---|---|
| 2 lbs. ground beef | 1 Tbsp salt |
| 2 c. cornbread crumbs | $^1/_4$ c. milk |
| $^3/_4$ c. minced onion | $^1/_4$ c. catsup (or thick tomato |
| $^1/_4$ c. chopped green pepper | pulp) |
| 2 eggs | 1 tsp dried mustard |
| 2 Tbsp horseradish | |

Mix all ingredients together, form into a loaf, and spread additional catsup on top. Bake at 400 degrees for 35 minutes. Makes 6 servings.

---

Glenn recalls that his mother hung strips of beef by the stovepipe of the wood cookstove to dry for about a week. Modern cooks can dry the beef in the stove in a slow oven.

### Creamed Dried Beef

Glenn Cardwell,
Greenbrier, TN

| | |
|---|---|
| Dried beef strips | 2 Tbsp flour |
| 2 Tbsp grease | 2 c. milk, approximately |

Prepare milk gravy by stirring flour into grease and adding milk until gravy is desired consistency. Add dried beef to gravy and pour over hot cornbread.

---

| | |
|---|---|
| Quail | 3 Tbsp melted butter |
| Lump of butter | $^1/_4$ tsp marjoram |
| $^1/_4$ c. water | |

### Roasted Quail

Ferne Shelton,
*Southern
Appalachian
Mountain
Cookbook*

Salt birds lightly. Place lump of butter inside each bird. Rub birds with mixture of flour and butter. Bake at 275 degrees for four hours. Make basting sauce of water, melted butter, and marjoram and baste bird frequently while cooking.

## Fried Quail (Bobwhite)

Duane Oliver,
*Cooking on Hazel Creek*

*Quail*
*2 Tbsp flour*

*2 c. milk*
*Salt*

Cut birds into serving size pieces, roll in seasoned flour, fry in hot grease until tender, turning once. Remove the meat and pour out all but two tablespoons of pan drippings. Stir in two tablespoons of flour and stir until light brown. Add about two cups of milk and cook, stirring until thickened. Add salt if needed. This same recipe can also be used to prepare grouse, dove, or turkey.

## Roast Wild Turkey

Duane Oliver,
*Cooking on Hazel Creek*

In the fall, turkeys began to eat the acorns and chestnuts, and any wild game that fattened on chestnuts was desirable food. They were hunted through the winter. Turkeys were more common when there were more openings in the forest.

*1 turkey*
*2 Tbsp salt*
*2 Tbsp pepper*
*1 Tbsp vinegar*
*3 stalks celery, diced*
*1 onion*

*1 potato, sliced*
*1/2 c. diced sweet pepper*
*1 stick margarine, melted*
*1/2 c. flour*
*2 quarts water*

Mix salt and pepper with vinegar, brush on outside and inside of bird. Combine celery, onion, potato, and sweet pepper and stuff into cavity of the bird. Mix butter and flour and brush on outside of bird. Place on rack in roaster and add water. Cover and bake at 350 degrees, 4 to 6 hours, basting with juice in pan until bird is browned and done.

Bear steak
Flour
White potatoes
$^1/_2$ c. water

1 tsp salt
1 onion, chopped
Pepper

**Bear Steak Stew**

Duane Oliver,
*Cooking on Hazel Creek*

Marinate the steak overnight, then dry and cut into small squares. Roll in flour and fry in fat until browned. Put the meat and some small potatoes in a dutch oven. Make mixture of the water, salt, onion, and pepper to taste and pour over the top. Cover and bake about $1^1/_2$ hours, adding more water as needed.

1 raccoon
3 tsp salt
3 c. sweet potatoes, mashed
$^3/_4$ c. raisins
$2^1/_2$ c. soft bread crumbs

$1^3/_4$ c. apples, diced
$^1/_3$ c. corn syrup
$^1/_4$ c. butter, melted
Salt and pepper

**Roast Coon with Sweet Potato Stuffing**

Duane Oliver,
*Cooking on Hazel Creek*

Remove the waxy nodules, called "kernels," from forelegs and from both sides of spine of a raccoon. Wash meat thoroughly and dry. Remove part of the fat, leaving just enough to cover the carcass with a thin layer. Sprinkle the body cavity with 1 teaspoon salt. Stuff with 2 teaspoons salt mixed with the mashed sweet potatoes, raisins, bread crumbs, apples, corn syrup, and melted butter. Skewer the vent closed, sprinkle with salt and pepper, and roast in oven, allowing about 45 minutes per pound of meat.

## Fried Venison (Deer)

Duane Oliver,
Cooking on Hazel Creek

| | |
|---|---|
| 2 lbs. venison (deer) steaks | One egg, beaten |
| $^1/_2$ c. vinegar | $^1/_2$ c. milk |
| Salt and pepper | Flour |

Place venison steaks in vinegar, add enough water to cover, and marinate for 1 hour. Rinse in cold water, season with salt and pepper. Mix the egg in milk. Dredge meat in flour, dip in egg mixture, and dredge in flour again. Brown in hot fat. Do not overcook.

## Mutton Stew

Duane Oliver,
Cooking on Hazel Creek

| | |
|---|---|
| 4 lbs. mutton | $^1/_4$ c. flour |
| Sugar | 6 c. boiling water |
| Fat | 2 potatoes |
| Salt and pepper | 10 small white onions |

Cut the mutton into small cubes. Sprinkle with a little sugar and fry in hot fat until brown on all sides. Season with salt and pepper. Stir in flour and cook until well browned. Gradually stir in the boiling water. Cover and simmer 1 hour. Add potatoes and onions, cover, and cook an hour longer.

## Vegetable Soup

Ferne Shelton,
Southern
Appalachian
Mountain
Cookbook

| | |
|---|---|
| 1 soup bone | $^1/_2$ c. turnips, diced |
| 3 quarts water | $^1/_2$ c. diced carrots |
| 2 c. tomatoes | 1 c. diced onions |
| 2 c. lima beans | Salt and pepper to taste |
| 2 c. corn | 1 tsp flour |
| 2 c. chopped cabbage | |

Wash soup bone thoroughly, add water and boil for several hours. Skim off excess fat and add vegetables and seasoning. Mix flour with $^1/_4$ cup water and add to soup. Cook for one hour.

Several squirrels
1 quart tomatoes
1 pint butter beans or limas
1 pint green corn
6 potatoes, parboiled and
    sliced
$^{1}/_{2}$ lb. butter

$^{1}/_{2}$ lb. salt pork
1 tsp black pepper
$^{1}/_{2}$ tsp cayenne
1 Tbsp salt
2 Tbsp white sugar
1 onion, minced small

**Brunswick
Stew**

Horace Kephart,
The Book of
Camping and
Woodcraft

Soak the squirrels half an hour in cold salted water. Add the salt to one gallon of water, and boil five minutes. Then put in the onion, beans, corn, pork (cut in fine strips), potatoes, pepper, and squirrels. Cover closely, and stew very slowly two and a half hours, stirring frequently. Add the tomatoes and sugar, and stew an hour longer. Then add the butter, cut into bits the size of a walnut and roll in flour. Boil ten minutes.

VEGETABLES & FRUITS

O F   T H E   S M O K I E S

Corn stalks
were cut and
piled in
"fodder
stacks" for
use in winter.
The Robert
Brown place
in
Cataloochee.
*1937 by C. S.
Grossman*

# VEGETABLES & FRUITS

"There's forty-eleven ways to use corn."
—Glenn Cardwell

To say corn was the staff of life for people of the Smokies is an understatement. Corn was the universal food—serving as both vegetable and grain—for mountain people everywhere. When times were hard, it was often the only thing that stood between them and starvation.

The golden grain has a long and noble heritage. Our common, everyday edible corn, *Zea mays*, most likely descended from a wild grass in Mexico and was domesticated perhaps 7,000 years ago. Corn's ancestry and path of migration northward from Mexico is an extremely complex story. Columbus took some back to Europe with him, and every schoolchild knows the story of the Indians' gift of corn to the Pilgrims during their first desperate winter at Plymouth Rock.

Corn is among the most versatile crops, adaptable and producing vigorously in a variety of climates and soils. It can be prepared and eaten in a manifold of forms—parched, popped, roasted, boiled, ground, or grated—and as mountaineers were well aware, distilled as an alcoholic drink. Corn is unusual in that the seeds, tightly enclosed within husks, cannot scatter and reseed themselves. Corn depends upon the hands of humans for planting, cultivation, and harvest.

When Europeans reached the Great Smoky Mountains, they found the resident Cherokee Indians cultivating corn, as native Americans had done for thousands of years in the New World. The Cherokees grew a flour corn, a traditional variety that modern geneticists think may be the only one of its kind in North America. Each year the Cherokees paid homage to Selu, the mother of corn, and held three major celebrations marking the different stages of corn planting and harvest. Superstitions and lore surrounded corn. The Cherokees dropped exactly seven grains of corn into each hill and never thinned the corn. Later settlers were of the belief that if corn came up missing in spots, it was a sign someone in the family would die within the year.

**Hard at work hoeing a "hard-scrabble" corn field.** *circa 1930 by Harry Wolfe courtesy Douglas Redding*

Upon their arrival, the European settlers' first order of business was clearing a piece of "newground" for the corn patch. They removed trees, stumps, and rocks, often girdling the trees to kill them. During the earliest days of settlement, corn was planted in hills among the stumps and tended entirely by hand. In the fertile land, they planted some wheat, rye, oats, and barley too, but corn was without exception the mainstay grain.

By 1840, Tennessee claimed fame as the leading corn producer in the country, winning the nickname of the "Hog and Hominy State." In 1849, several farmers in the Oconaluftee River valley on the North Carolina side of the Smokies reported raising a thousand bushels of corn.

Every spring, or more often in late winter, a farmer hitched his steadfast workhorse to the plow and readied the field for planting once again. The 180-day growing season in the mountains is shorter than the Deep South, so a Smokies farmer normally waited at least until April or even May to plant corn, to avoid a killing frost. Seed corn, carefully saved from the best ears of the previous year's harvest, was dropped into the furrows.

During the steamy days of summer, corn had to be hoed, usually three or four times before it was waist high. When the hoeing was completed, the corn was then said to be "laid

Cherokee woman demonstrates hominy making. *by Jim Ayres*

by," possibly by midsummer depending upon when it was planted. For a few days in late summer, fresh corn was prime for roasted, or "rosen," ears. The ears were plucked off the stalks and roasted in fireplace coals, or shucked and placed on oven racks in a stove. There are also those who plunge fresh shucked ears into a pot of boiling water, without wasting a minute from field to plate. Slathered with country butter, fresh corn on the cob, roasted or boiled, was a true feast. Past the roasting ear stage, the milky kernels were grated off the cob and baked into a mountain specialty, "gritted bread," or a cook might stir up a "run" of cornmeal mush.

Well into autumn, the rest of the ear corn was harvested, stacked on a sled or wagon, and hauled to the corncrib where it would stay dry for milling. The corncrib, which held a good portion of the family's wealth, was a place to be guarded. According to an acquaintance of Roaring Fork resident Ephraim Bales, "old Eph kept his rifle hangin' right here over the window. If he heard the shutter squeak on the corn crib, he took his rifle down." That dry corn in the crib could be parched, ground into cornmeal, made into hominy, or occasionally fed to the animals.

The hands-down favorite variety of corn all over the Smokies was Hickory King, also called Hickory Cane. This large-kerneled, eight-row, white dent corn was introduced commercially in the mid 1800s and was favored because it made the best hominy and cornmeal for bread. Even today, many mountain gardeners plant a patch of tall, lanky Hickory King for old times' sake, and because they still like to eat it.

Hickory King bears one or two ears on each stalk, and the tight husks are insect resistant. It is an open-pollinated corn, relying on the wind to spread the pollen, and thus didn't require the attention of the new hybrids introduced in the 1930s. Hybrid sweet corn did prove popular for roasting ears though. Most any day in July, an old Ford pickup parks along a road into the park, the bed of the truck loaded with fresh-picked corn still in the husks; the farmer puts out a hand-lettered cardboard sign advertising "CORN," likely Silver Queen or another sweet hybrid. A one-dollar bill will get you a dozen ears.

Still, most mountain folk would not consider making hominy with anything but Hickory King. Hominy—cooked whole corn with the hulls off the kernels—was a culinary staple for both the Cherokees and Euro-American settlers in the Smokies. Making hominy is an age-old process. Ashes (preferably hickory) were taken from the fireplace. (In most households, people weren't allowed to spit in the fireplace to assure the ashes were clean.) The ashes were put into a wooden ash hopper and water poured through them to make lye. The lye and corn were put into an old pot with plenty of water and boiled until the hulls slipped off the kernels and the corn was snowy white. The water was changed two or three times until clear. This swollen corn—canned, pickled, or dried—would be fried in bacon drippings and eaten for dinner or supper. The addition of alkali-rich wood ash was a major step in improving corn's nutritional value. The alkali provided niacin, a mineral lacking in corn.

In the past, farmers went into their fields in mid September to cut the tops off the corn. It was a hot, itchy chore, in which the tops, stalk and all, were removed just above the highest ear. These were tied in bundles and stacked. After the tops dried, they were fed to the milk cows during the winter. Farmers also "pulled fodder," that is, removed the leaves from the stalks and fed them to the cows, horses, and sheep.

Soft, crinkly corn shucks were put to every imaginable use—stuffed into mattresses, woven into chair seats, made into mops and brushes, braided into horse collars and harnesses, and fashioned into delightful dolls. The cobs were used for stove kindling, and cobs from varieties other than Hickory King made good smoking pipes.

All the planting, harvesting, and shucking were done by hand, and these events provided as good excuse as any for festive, social gatherings. A common practice at corn huskings was to pile the corn high in the barnyard, bury a half gallon of liquor down in it, then call the neighbors to come shuck the corn and locate the prize. Or, the first person to find a red ear of corn got various rewards: a kiss, a dance, or a Jersey cow. After all this hard work, it was time to break out the fiddles and sing the whole night long.

Often, bean plants curled up the twelve-foot-tall stalks of Hickory King. The corn stalks provided stout trellises for pole beans, and this happy co-planting also gave the corn a good dose of nitrogen from nodules on the roots of the beans. (Additional garden fertilizer consisted of barnyard manure and ashes from the fireplace.)

Smoky Mountain horticulture includes a lengthy litany of legumes—creasebacks, cutshorts, cornfield beans, bunch beans, pink or peanut beans, greasy beans, sulfur beans, and half runners. There were red-streaked October beans, the Lazy Wife's pole bean, the Blue Ribbon bean, and the Turkey Craw bean, said to have been taken from the craw of a turkey by a hunter. Others carry the names of the people who first grew or commercialized them, like the big pole bean with a white seed called a White McCaslin. Lucinda Ogle of Gatlinburg remembered one called MinWin, a bean named for her Aunt Minnie Win who "kept seed for everybody." And as with Hickory King corn, some of these beans qualify today as heirlooms, passed generously from the hands of one gardener to another and cultivated by serious seed savers who want to preserve this genetic wealth.

Basically, beans can be divided into two groups—pole beans that grow tall and bush beans that grow closer to the ground. Some were eaten as fresh green beans, while others were canned or shelled and dried for winter use. Leather britches, also called shuck beans or fodder beans, are still popular. These beans are strung and dried and then rehydrated for consumption.

In late fall, cooked beans, corn, or both mixed together were covered in a salty brine, and stored in crocks, barrels, or canned in jars to be eaten throughout the winter. If a wooden barrel was the vessel, the seams were sealed with beeswax to keep the liquids from leaking out. Heavy brown stoneware crocks were also indispensable for preserving and storing pickled beans and corn, as well as cucumber pickles, sauerkraut, and sulphured apples. Going into winter, a family would want at least a sixty-gallon barrel of each of these, maybe two barrels of sulphured apples for a large family.

Potatoes were the third essential vegetable grown in gardens all over the Smoky Mountains. There were several kinds: the white Irish potato or Cobbler, Blue Goose, Pontiac, and the sweet potato. The so-called Irish potato is actually a native of the Andes of South America, cultivated in Peru since at least 750 B.C. Potatoes were brought to Ireland in 1565, and Sir Francis Drake carried them to England thirty years later.

Potatoes made their way back across the ocean in the 1600s, to the colonies along the Atlantic Seaboard.

Because potatoes grew underground, the Irish could keep them from the hands of the landlord's tax collector, who would not deign to dig in the ground to seize them. Potatoes were good, filling fare, and people soon added them to their diet. The Irish, however, paid dearly for their almost exclusive reliance on potatoes. When blight struck the crop in the 1840s, at least a million Irish died in the resulting famine.

In March, usually, Smokies gardeners cut up seed potatoes, with one eye or two per piece, and put them in the ground. A ridge of soil would be built up around the plants as they started to come up. One old saying declared the land was so steep potatoes could be planted in rows going up and down the mountain instead of around it. This made harvest easy, because the potatoes could all just roll downhill.

Steep the land may be, but it grows Irish potatoes as big as two softballs. A person could just go out to the garden and "grabble out" as many as needed for a meal. After the final harvest, potatoes were stored in "tater holes" dug under the cabin floor, often near the hearth, reached by lifting a board in the floor. Others buried potatoes near the house in a hay-lined hole covered with a board or piece of tin.

According to Tennessean Hubert Sullivan, "you plant potatoes on the old moon, but you want to dig 'em on the new moon, they keep better." Many mountaineers religiously observed the signs of the zodiac and the phases of the moon to tell them when to plant certain crops. They planted according to signs associated with the head, loins, feet, knees, and so on. Root or underground crops, for example, were planted when the signs were in the feet and the moon was waning; beans were to be planted when the signs were in the arms. For aboveground crops such as corn, people waited until the moon was waxing, or growing; corn planted in a new moon wouldn't produce well and would grow so high you couldn't reach the ears. They observed other signs as well: some might wait to hear the first whippoorwill calling, or check the leaves on the oaks to see if they had

*Boil a biscuit with cabbage and there will be no odor.*

**Peeling apples and other types of food preparation work were often social activities.**
*courtesy Appalachian Collection, Mars Hill College, NC*

reached the size of a squirrel's ear. According to Bonnie Myers, who grew up in Cades Cove, muskmelons had to be planted on the tenth of May, two seeds per hill. Others would plant a garden on the hundredth day of the calendar year, or on Good Friday. Both practices invoked religious blessings. These "rules" seemed to vary from one person to another, however. What one would swear by, another might swear just the opposite, and some people disavowed them altogether and planted when the time seemed right.

Along with corn, beans, and potatoes, a whole constellation of other garden vegetables was cultivated: beets, peas, parsnips, turnips, cabbage, lettuce, onions, squash, pumpkins, melons, cucumbers, tomatoes, and peppers. Some, such as scallions and red onions, were "treasures you bargained and swapped with people," said Lucinda Ogle. The old field or clay peas people grew in their gardens were thrashed out of the hulls by putting the dried peas on a sheet laid out on the porch and beating them with flat sticks. Peas cooked with molasses were called baked "beans."

Turnips were planted twice a year, in spring for the greens and in autumn for the underground tubers. When turnip greens, cabbage, or the like were cooked, the liquid that remained was called "pot likker," a rich substance never discarded but always savored for cornbread dipping. Cabbage was a good cool-weather vegetable that was easy to store right in the garden: the plants were pulled up, placed upside down in a trench next to the row, covered with leaves and dirt, and simply left in the ground. Cabbage was made into fresh coleslaw for a summer picnic, fermented in a crock for sauerkraut, or chopped fine and pickled in an interesting relish called chowchow. To add spice to this bounty of produce, every garden had an herb row with garlic, sage, horseradish, dill, and mint.

Along with vegetables came fruit, and in the mountains that most often meant apples. The forbidden fruit of this member of the rose family was eaten fresh and fixed in countless ways: fried, dried, bleached (sulphured), baked in cakes, and as pie timber, not to mention apple butter, applesauce, apple jelly, apple cider, and its fermented descendant, vinegar.

Apple varieties grown in the old days are ones mostly unknown today. They included Limbertwigs, Milams, Sheepnose, Sour Johns and Winter Johns, Early Harvest, Grimes Golden, Rusty Sweets, Summer Rambos, Buckinghams, Banana Apples, and June Apples. Older mountain folk long for their incomparable taste, writing letters to local newspapers asking if anyone knows where they might find them. Orchardist John Dunn tends apple trees in Dry Valley, near Townsend, Tennessee, in the same place where his father, L.P. Dunn, had his orchard. John Dunn recalled a number of other disappearing varieties, including the late summer Beard Apple, Yellow Transparents, York Imperials, a tart Hog Apple, the North Carolina Horse Apple, and the dark-skinned Arkansas Black.

Apples and other fruit were sliced and dried on a wooden scaffold, in a kiln, or simply by laying out on rocks. Lucinda Ogle holds clear childhood memories of "Granny's drying rock" near the Noah "Bud" Ogle cabin. They placed the ripe peaches on a sheet on the big, flat boulder, and if rain threatened, Lucinda had to gather up the fruit in the sheet and bring it inside. (Lucinda's rock, by the way, can still be seen near the Noah "Bud" Ogle cabin.) Once glass "cans" arrived, spiced peaches were put up, a little bit of summer in a jar. Sweet peach butter was a fine addition to hot biscuits. Rhubarb was a

*Sun-drying was one of the most common ways of preserving fruits and vegetables.*

garden fruit that came in early. The stems were chopped and stewed into a sauce that wouldn't hurt a biscuit at all.

After a winter of dried fruit, salted meat, and starchy potatoes, the first sprigs of green poking up through the dull duff of the forest floor were a glad sight. Many of these wild greens are edible and rich in vitamins. Ramps, poke, dock, violets, dandelions, and cresses (or creases, both wet and dryland) were among the most common. They were fixed in fresh salads or cooked as potherbs and valued as "spring tonics."

The woods and fields and streambanks of the Smokies are blessed with so many different kinds of wild herbs a person had to know what was safe to eat. "We'd go with Granny," said Lucinda Ogle, "and she'd show us what to get. We had wild cress that grew in fields, wild mustard early in the spring, little new dock leaves, and lamb's quarters." Brook lettuce was fried in bacon fat. And in spring, nearly every table hosted a mess of poke "sallet"—the cooked, young leaves of pokeweed.

Ramps were another highly sought delicacy, their thin lilylike leaves sprouting in buckeye flats, along shaded creeks, and beneath maple trees. The young leaves were put in salads; when the plants were larger, the bulbs were eaten raw like onions. These strong-flavored, strong-scented wild leeks weren't recommended for a couple that was a'courtin. The appearance of ramps is still celebrated each April at the Ramp Festival in Cosby, Tennessee, where a Ramp Queen is crowned as people munch on fried chicken with a side dish of ramps and scrambled eggs. Most of these same wild greens were known to the Cherokees, and undoubtedly they introduced many of them to the pioneers. The Indians gathered ramps from March through April and May, ate the bulb raw, parboiled the entire plant, or chopped them up with fried eggs. Another Cherokee favorite was *sochani*, the early shoots and leaves of the green-headed coneflower. The greenery was cut, peeled, quartered, and boiled with several changes of water, then fried in a large amount of fat, similar to the way pokeweed was prepared. The Cherokees also parboiled or fried the tender young leaves of beargrass and ate branch lettuce as a salad with other vegetables. Young Solomon's seal was boiled and fried, along with lovage, spiderwort, cowcress, yellow rocket, early cress, shepherd's purse, pigweed and lamb's quarters, crow's foot, self heal, and dock.

As spring passed into summer and Queen Anne's lace and black-eyed Susans graced the roadsides, it was berry picking

## Homecoming Menu

Fried Chicken

Country Ham

Green Beans & Onions

Fried Squash

Fresh Tomatoes

Pickled Beets

Pickled Peaches

Potato Salad

Deviled Eggs

Ham Biscuits

Cornbread

Chocolate Cake

Apple Pie

Egg Custard Pie

time. The mountains were thick with all kinds of berries—
blackberries, bearberries, gooseberries, huckleberries, blueberries, elderberries, raspberries, serviceberries, and wild
strawberries. As anyone knows who's ever savored wild
strawberries, they bear no comparison to the big, nearly tasteless
ones sold in stores today. Hubert Sullivan remembered another
one—the dewberry. They grew on a vine and were much like a
blackberry with large seeds. "I ain't seen 'em in years," said
Hubert. Other wild fruits available for the
picking included crab apples, wild
cherries, and wild plums.

Buena Winchester and her brothers
went to the berry patch with ten-quart
galvanized buckets. When the four of
them had heaped eight of those buckets
high with berries, they'd carry them back
to the house and her mother would start
canning them. Then she and the boys
would go back and pick more, enough to
fill 100 or 200 half-gallon canning jars.

Open clearings and road edges are
still tangled with the canes of blackberries
drooping with jeweled purple fruits, and
many mountain residents set out with tin

John Gregory
shows off one
of the
pleasures of
summer.
*courtesy Randolph
Shields*

buckets and berry baskets to reap this luscious wealth. A trip to
the berry patch demands a long-sleeved shirt and long trousers,
and tolerance of some discomfort. The hazy heat of July rises as
the morning wears on; you sweat, swat bugs, scratch your hands
on thorns, and keep a watchful eye out for berry-gobbling bears.
But it's all worthwhile as the juicy morsels start to fill the bucket.
It's impossible not to sample a few, of course, and that burst of
sweet, wild flavor conjures fantasies, soon to be realized, of
blackberry cobblers, blackberry dumplings, and blackberry jam.

Around old homesites and fields in the lowlands of the
Smokies are found tall elderberry bushes. In June and July the
shrubs bear big clumps of white flowers the old-timers called
"elder blow." These hearty blossoms can be dipped in batter and

fried in oil as a fritter. By August, clusters of deep purple berries appear. Fresh elderberries must be cooked to be usable in jelly, juice, or wine. When dried, the berries' sweetness is concentrated, and they are delicious in muffins and pies.

Cherokee oral history tells how strawberries came to the people. A woman, angry at her husband, left her home one day. Her husband prayed to the Great One, who tried to stop the woman by putting berry bushes in her path. First he put serviceberry, then huckleberry, but she ignored them both. Then he put a small plant at ground level, its leaves hiding a sweet-smelling fruit. When the wife stumbled upon these, her curiosity was aroused. She forgot her anger and picked the biggest, ripest red berries to take back to her husband. When they met, she put one in his mouth, and then they both started picking the berries. The husband decided that to keep his wife forever he would plant a patch of strawberries near their home. She wondered how she could have ever left her home, and determined always to keep a jar of preserved strawberries as a reminder how fragile home is and how powerful anger can be.

As the berries faded, nuts began showering down from the trees. People had to gather nuts quickly before the squirrels, birds, and other animals got them all. Walnuts, hickory nuts, hazelnuts, butternuts, acorns, and in the past, chestnuts, were carted home by the bushelfuls. Nuts were hulled, dried, and shelled for use in baked goods.

The chestnut was one of the most highly valued trees of the forest, its burr-covered seed pods reliably producing brown nuts every year. Chestnuts were gathered and hauled in wagons to market in towns such as Knoxville, often a multiday excursion in former days. The sale of the nuts provided an important cash crop for Smokies residents. Chestnut bread was a staple of the Cherokees, and chestnuts were eaten whole and roasted, and cooked in soups, stews, vegetable dishes, and desserts.

The passing of the chestnut was mourned by Indian and non-Indian alike, anyone who remembered with fondness the time when these fine trees graced the deep coves of the Smokies forest. At the turn of the century, a parasitic Asian fungus

*Possum up a 'simmon tree, Raccoon on the ground. Coon say to the possum, boy, Shake them 'simmons down!*

*Possum 'gan to shake the tree, 'Simmons 'gan to fall. Coon say to the possum, boy, I didn't want 'em all!*

arrived in the United States. The blight reached the Smokies in the mid 1920s, and by 1935 nearly all the chestnut trees in the park had been killed. One remaining stand was producing nuts in 1938, but by the early 1940s the harvest of chestnuts had ended in the Smoky Mountains. Determined efforts to resurrect the American chestnut have not yet born fruit; the chestnuts we buy and eat today are imported, mostly from Italy.

Autumn is also the time when fox grapes, possum grapes, persimmons, and pawpaws ripen, along with many edible mushrooms. Persimmons were eaten raw or in pies and puddings; green persimmons pack real pucker power so it was wise to wait until after a hard frost to harvest them. The same is true of the pawpaw, or custard apple, which grows on a shrub or small tree in moist woods and along creeks. When yellowish-brown, the fruit is ripe and tastes like a cross between a banana and a mango. Children trailed down to the pawpaw patch after school and ate them fresh off the trees for a snack. Or, pawpaws were baked in breads or custards. Maypops, the seedy fruit of the passion flower, were called old field apricots; the Cherokees made them into a drink while others ate them raw or cooked them into jellies and preserves.

## Hominy

Bessie Jumper,
Little Snowbird, NC

This is an old Cherokee recipe, taken from an interview with Bessie Jumper from Museum of the Cherokee archives.

*Flour corn, about 1/2 gallon*   *1 c. walnuts*
*Lye water*   *1/3 c. cornmeal*
*Pinto beans*

Mix about 6–8 cups of ashes (oak and hickory are best) with cold water in a pot, not too thick; when this boils, pour in corn. Boil corn in lye water only to hard boil, and as you stir the skin comes off the corn. After it's done, wash the corn real good, wash all the ashes off, and boil corn again for 2–3 hours. Just before it's done, put in pinto beans and cook with corn. When both are cooked, pour in the walnuts and cornmeal, mixed together and beat fine with hammer or mortar and pestle pounder. This pounder is made of oak, a short log hollowed out on one end like a bowl, the pestle about two inches at one end and six inches in diameter at other end. The small end fits into opening in log where corn is ground or pounded.

---

## Hominy Soup

Mollie
Runningwolfe
Sequoyah,
Big Cove, NC,
*Cherokee Cooklore*

*Hominy corn*      *Lye water from wood ashes*

Use hominy corn to make hominy soup. Put the corn in lye until the skin slips. Beat corn in the corn beater, then sift the meal to remove larger particles. Cook these larger pieces in water until done. Store soup in pottery jar, and it will turn sour like buttermilk by the next day. May be kept four days before discarding. This drink was always served to visitors and to people working in fields.

---

## Mush
## A-Ni-S-Ta

Mollie
Runningwolfe
Sequoyah,
Big Cove, NC,
*Cherokee Cooklore*

While plain water comes to boil in pot, wet cornmeal with a little cold water. Add the wet meal slowly to the boiling water and stir until done.

Flour corn
Lye from wood ashes
Colored beans
Pumpkin

Cornmeal
Hickory nuts and walnuts
Molasses

## Corn & Beans
Se-Lu A-Su-Yi Tu-Yu

Mrs. Clifford
Hornbuckle,
Cherokee Cooklore

Skin flour corn with lye, then cook. Cook colored beans. Put the cooked corn and beans together and cook some more. (You may add pumpkin, but be sure to cook until pumpkin is done). Add to this a mixture of cornmeal, beaten walnuts and hickory nuts, and enough molasses to sweeten. Cook in an iron pot until the meal is done. May be eaten fresh or after it begins to sour. It will not keep after souring unless weather is cold.

A variation is fried corn and beans: Cook skinned corn and colored beans separately, then put together and cook some more. Add a little grease and set aside to cool. When firm, slice and fry in hot grease.

---

Corn
Lye ashes

Green beans
Pumpkin (optional)

## Succotash
I-Ya-Tsu-Ya-Di-Su-Yi Se-Lu

Agnes Catolster,
Cherokee, NC,
Cherokee Cooklore

Shell some corn, skin it with wood ashes lye. Cook corn and green beans separately, then together. If desired, pieces of pumpkin may be added, but be sure to put in pumpkin in time to get done before the pot is removed from the fire.

---

1 gallon large kernel
corn

1 quart hardwood ashes
(makes the lye)

## Homemade Hominy

Martha Whaley,
Gatlinburg, TN,
Gatlinburg Recipe
Collection

Cover corn with water. Tie ashes in muslin and cook with corn until skin or husk slips off when pressed between thumb and forefinger. Remove ashes and wash corn through three waters. Cook for one hour, then wash again. Repeat this three times, or until all lye is removed. Cook until corn is soft, about six hours.

**Hominy**

John D. Webb,
Townsend, TN

Use 2 tablespoons of commercial lye to a gallon of corn. Put in a big iron kettle, cover with water, and boil until husks come off kernels. Pour cold water on, dip off husks, rinse 8–10 times through clean water. Cook until done. Fry hominy in skillet with bacon grease.

To make hominy these days, commercial lye can be used instead of lye made from wood ashes. Household lye is the only one suitable for food use, in proportions of one teaspoonful per quart of water. Be aware that lye is a caustic substance that requires EXTREME CAUTION when handling. If lye comes into contact with skin, wash immediately with cold water followed by vinegar, or boric acid solution if it gets into eyes. To make hominy, use only iron or enamel kettles, never aluminum.

**Parched Corn**

Thelma Phillips,
Norris, TN

Shell dried field corn and place in ungreased skillet. Cook slowly, about two hours or so, on top of stove, in oven, or on rock in front of fireplace. Crunchy kernels can be eaten out of hand, or ground up for coffee substitute.

---

**Pickled Corn**

Mrs. Ollie
Lawhern,
Maryville-Alcoa
Times

*Ear corn*                          *Salt*

Steam ears of corn in hot water for a few minutes to set the milk. Cut the corn from the cob. Mix four parts corn with one part pure salt. Put in crock, weigh down with dish, cover with cloth, set in cool place. Let "work" 3–5 weeks. Remove as much as you need, freshen by soaking in cold water, repeat until corn tastes sweet. Cook until tender, season to taste. Serve with milk and butter.

Corn                    Salt

**Pickled Corn**

Bonnie Myers,
Townsend, TN

In the fall, when cool weather arrives, select an armload of fresh corn. Shuck the ears, remove damaged ends, silks, and thin shucks. Cook until done in big dishpan or pot. When cooled, cut corn off cob into a large pan. Add a cup of salt. Stir well. Put into clean, sterile quart canning jars. Fill jars with boiling water. Seal and store in cool, dark place. This corn was also put into crockware and stored outside during winter.

---

Corn                    Salt
Beans

**Pickled Corn & Beans**

Beuna Winchester,
Bryson City, NC

Corn and beans were pickled late in the fall so they would keep through the winter. Beuna Winchester's family always pickled beans in sixty-gallon wooden barrels they kept in the springhouse, as well as a sixty-gallon barrel of corn and beans mixed—a gallon of beans to each gallon of corn. Canning salt was used to make the brine.

Make a sack out of white cloth to fit inside a ten-gallon crock. Pack beans and corn in the sack, then pour salt water over it, close the sack, and weigh down with plate and a river rock.

A mold will gather on top of the salt water, but it is not a problem. Simply move the rock, pick up sack, remove the mold and rinse off. "I don't think it hurts you, but it don't look good," said Beuna.

(To make smaller quantities, use about 3/4 cup salt to a gallon of water, and cover corn or beans with brine solution.)

To pickle corn on the cob: Fill a big old crock full of corn on the cob, and add a little extra salt because the cob absorbs salt. Cut kernels off the cob to cook it. To prepare, get desired amount from the barrel or crock and fry like sauerkraut.

## Pickled Beans

Mrs. Ollie Lawhern, *Maryville-Alcoa Times*

| Green beans | Vinegar |
| Salt | Dill weed |

Wash green beans and snap, or break, beans into one- or two-inch-long pieces. Put them in some water and boil about 10 minutes. Add salt as if you were going to eat them. Then skim out the beans and put in crock. Cover with boiling vinegar sweetened and spiced to taste. A bit of "dilley weed" makes them pretty good.

## Fresh Green Beans

Nancy Cooper, Gatlinburg, TN, *Gatlinburg Recipe Collection*

| 3 lbs. fresh green beans | 1 tsp salt |
| 3 thick slices of salt pork | 1 hot pepper (optional) |
| 1 whole small onion | Salt |

Remove strings from whole green beans and snap the beans into one-inch pieces. Wash beans in cold water. Heat heavy pot on stove eye and add salt pork. Brown pork on each side, add about $1/2$ c. water, add green beans and onion for seasoning. Add salt and hot pepper. Cover and simmer about $2^1/2$–3 hours. Check beans while cooking and add more water if needed, enough water just to keep beans from burning. When beans are done, set off stove and remove onion. Good left over—refrigerate and reheat.

## Southern Green Beans

Louise Woodruff, Walland, TN

"Mom would put them on of a morning just after breakfast and she would wash her beans and put her meat in and her salt and she'd cook them slowly until twelve o'clock, until dinner."

| 2 quarts green beans | 1 tsp salt |
| 3-inch square bacon | |

String and cut beans in 1-inch pieces, wash, crisp in cold water one hour. Add beans to boiling, salted water, add bacon and just enough water to cover. When beans are tender, remove bacon and finish cooking.

"They ain't good without grease in 'em, a bone's better than anything, if you've got a hambone lay it in over beans."

## Leather Britches

Beuna Winchester,
Bryson City, NC

*Half runner beans*                    *Hambone*

Snap half runner beans into good-sized pieces and string them with needle and twine or strong thread. They color better if hung out of the sun in a loft or attic. Dry until they're "brickle" (brittle), then store in bags or pillow cases.

To cook leather britches, soak the dry beans at least 12 hours to rehydrate them, then put on to cook slow. They get better every time they are rewarmed. Expect the dry beans to expand about three times in volume when they are cooked.

---

*Stick beans*                    *Streaked pork*

## Leather Britches Beans

Bonnie Myers,
Townsend, TN

Wash and thread late-summer stick beans and hang in attic to dry during winter. Break up beans and soak overnight. The next morning, drain and add fresh water to cover, two or three inches in heavy pot. Add three, quarter-inch strips of streaked pork. Cook slowly two to three hours or until tender.

---

John D. Webb raises a glorious garden behind his home in Townsend. His beans are the one dish no Smokies potluck can do without.

## John D.'s Beans

John D. Webb,
Townsend, TN

*4 lbs. dry pinto and
    great northern beans*

*4 oz. salt bacon
Salt and pepper*

Wash and soak beans for a couple of hours. Put in big pot and cover with water. Add bacon. Cook until done, about $2^{1}/_{2}$–3 hours. You don't have to stir the beans, but make sure they don't run out of water. Add salt and pepper to taste.

## Baked Beans

Louise Woodruff,
Walland, TN

3 c. white beans
3/4 lb. fresh salt pork
1 Tbsp prepared mustard
1 tsp ginger

2 Tbsp molasses
Salt and pepper to taste
1 Tbsp brown sugar

Soak beans overnight. Rinse and drain in morning. Cover with cold water, boil 15 minutes. Drain. Put beans in buttered baking dish; add other ingredients and sliced pork, scalded. Place pork in beans with rind exposed. Cover with boiling water, bake 6 hours. Remove cover for last 30 minutes to brown.

## Myrell & Wiley's Bean & Bacon Soup

Myrell Ballew
Moore, in Duane
Oliver,
Cooking on Hazel
Creek

1/2 lb. navy beans
1 small onion, chopped
1/2 c. celery, chopped

Salt to taste
6 slices bacon

Soak beans for 2 hours in cold water. Drain and wash with cold water. Return beans to pot, cover with water and cook about 45 minutes. Add onion, celery, and salt and cook 30 minutes longer or until beans are done. Fry bacon until crisp. Cool and crumble into soup. Let simmer a few minutes before serving.

## Nine Day Slaw

Lucinda Ogle,
Gatlinburg, TN

3 lbs. cabbage, shredded
1 green pepper, chopped

2 onions, sliced

Mix and bring to boil:

1 c. sugar
1 c. vinegar
1 c. oil

2 tsp salt
2 tsp dry mustard

Pour hot liquid mixture over cabbage and other vegetables, stirring well. Place in refrigerator overnight. This slaw can be used for nine days, hence its name.

*1 tsp salt*
*1 tsp sugar*
*1 tsp vinegar*

*Chopped cabbage, one head*
*per quart*
*1 pod hot red pepper*

### Sauerkraut

Beuna Winchester,
Bryson City, NC

Sterilize quart jars and lids. Measure ¹/₂ teaspoon of salt in bottom of each jar. Fill each jar with cabbage, coarsely chopped, then add the sugar, vinegar, and the other ¹/₂ teaspoon of salt. Don't pack too tightly. Pour boiling water to cover, leaving adequate headroom. Put lid on tight, wrap in newspaper, and place in cool place. Beuna puts hers on bottom shelf in basement. Kraut will ferment and is ready to eat in 6–8 weeks.

---

*Sauerkraut*
*Pork or ham hock*

*Biscuit dough*

### Sauerkraut Dumplings

Elsie Burrell,
Maryville, TN

Cook sauerkraut with fresh pork or ham hock, bring to boil, drop biscuit dough into boiling kraut and let boil about 10 minutes. If you have big crowd, you can cut up and add potatoes.

*1 small head cabbage*
*Fat*

*1 tsp hot red pepper*
*Salt*

### Smoky Fried Cabbage

Beuna Winchester,
Bryson City, NC

Wash and shred cabbage, heat fat in iron skillet, put the cabbage in, stir until cabbage is shiny. Lower heat, add red pepper and salt, and continue cooking until cabbage is tender.

## Coleslaw

Mrs. Ollie
Lawhern,
Maryville-Alcoa
Times

Cabbage
Bacon fat
Sugar

Vinegar
Salt and pepper to taste

Cut cabbage into small pieces and put in a bowl. Melt some bacon fat in a skillet, put in some sugar and vinegar, cook to boiling. When hot, pour dressing over cabbage, mix in a hurry, and serve. Can add pinch or two of salt and big dash of pepper if you like.

---

## Twenty-Four Hour Slaw

Louise Woodruff,
Walland, TN

1 cabbage
1 onion
1 pepper
1 carrot
1 c. sugar

1 c. vinegar
1 c. oil
1 Tbsp powdered mustard
  or seed
$1/2$ tsp salt

Chop vegetables in a bowl. Bring sugar, vinegar, oil, mustard, and salt to a boil and pour over cabbage mixture.

---

## Slaw

Bonnie Myers,
Townsend, TN

Small head cabbage
$1/4$ c. vinegar
White sugar

$1/3$ c. cold water
Dash salt
Dash black pepper

Peel and wash the cabbage. Remove stalk and shred or chop cabbage. Add vinegar, water, salt and pepper, and sweeten to taste with sugar.

---

## Turnip Slaw

Lois Caughron,
Cades Cove, TN

3 c. shredded turnip
$1 1/2$ c. shredded carrot
$1/2$ c. raisins, optional
1 Tbsp lemon juice

$1/2–3/4$ c. of mayonnaise, or
  dressing of vinegar, salt,
  water, sugar, and pepper

Combine all ingredients in large bowl. Stir well. Cover and chill.

Lettuce — Fat

This simple recipe calls for pouring hot grease over garden lettuce, thus "killing" its crispness. It was a good old-time way to fix a salad.

---

2 eggs
¹/₂ tsp mustard (made mustard by beating seeds from greens)
¹/₂ tsp salt
¹/₈ tsp paprika

¹/₈ tsp pepper
2 Tbsp sugar
2 Tbsp flour
1 Tbsp butter
1 c. water
¹/₃ c. vinegar

**Cooked Salad Dressing**

Beat eggs and sift dry ingredients into them. Add butter. Gradually stir in water and vinegar. Cook in double boiler until dressing coats the spoon. Remove from fire at once and chill before using.

---

Small white onions
2 Tbsp grease or butter
2 Tbsp flour

1 c. milk
Salt to taste

**Creamed Onions**

Duane Oliver, *Cooking on Hazel Creek*

Simmer small white onions until tender. Drain and make a white gravy of butter or grease, flour, milk, and salt. Add onions and simmer until warmed through.

---

2 Tbsp sugar
2 Tbsp cornstarch or flour
¹/₄ c. water

³/₄ c. vinegar
4 c. cooked beets
Butter (optional)

**Harvard Beets**

Lucinda Ogle, Gatlinburg, TN

Mix sugar and cornstarch; add vinegar and water. Cook 5 minutes, stirring to prevent lumping. Add beets and cook until thoroughly heated. Can also add 2 tablespoons of butter.

## Boiled Turnips

Mrs. Ollie Lawhern, Maryville-Alcoa Times

18–20 turnips                     Butter
Salt and pepper

Dig turnips from the turnip hole. Wash, peel, and cut them. Put in pot and just cover with water. Cook until tender. Pour off water and mash them or leave them whole. Season with salt and pepper and lots of butter.

## Parsnips

Bonnie Myers, Townsend, TN

Plant parsnips in late April for fall use.

Parsnips                          Chunk of butter size of egg
$^1/_2$ tsp salt                  Sugar
Water

Wash and peel parsnips. Slice. Put into medium heavy pot. Add salt. Barely cover with water. Add butter along with several pinches of sugar to taste. Cook slowly until tender.

## Sweet Potatoes

Mrs. Ollie Lawhern, Maryville-Alcoa Times

Rub each potato with lard and place in front of fire or in pan in the oven. Roast 'til soft and steamy. Remove and serve with lots of butter and sorghum molasses.

## Yam Souffle

Beuna Winchester, Bryson City, NC

4 c. mashed North Carolina        3 eggs, beaten
   yams                           $^1/_4$ tsp salt
$^1/_2$ c. butter, softened       $^1/_4$ c. black walnuts, chopped
$^1/_2$ c. sugar

In large mixing bowl, beat together yams, butter, sugar, eggs, and salt until fluffy. Turn into baking dish and sprinkle with walnuts. Bake at 350 degrees for 45 minutes. Serve immediately. Serves 6.

Salt pork or bacon, 6–7
slices
Green tomatoes

Milk
Grease
Flour seasoned with salt and
pepper

### Paw's Fried Green Tomatoes

Beuna Winchester,
Bryson City, NC

Fry up salt pork or bacon and set in warm place. Slice tomatoes $^1/_2$ inch thick. Dip in seasoned flour. Fry in meat grease until brown on both sides. Remove tomatoes to hot platter and put in warm place. Pour off all except 2 tablespoons of drippings and thicken with flour, add milk, and boil into gravy. Top the fried tomatoes with the slices of salt pork and pour on the gravy. Some folks use ripe tomatoes, but "Paw" liked green ones best.

1 lb. okra, cleaned
and sliced
$^1/_2$ c. flour

$^1/_2$ c. cornmeal
Salt and pepper
Oil

### Fried Okra

Duane Oliver,
Cooking on Hazel
Creek

Mix flour, cornmeal, salt, and pepper. Roll okra in this mixture and fry in hot oil until golden brown, about 7 minutes. Drain and serve.

Irish potatoes
Onion, chopped
Bell pepper

Vinegar
2 eggs, hard-boiled
Salt

### Potato Salad

Bonnie Myers,
Townsend, TN

Cook small to medium potatoes unpeeled. Peel when cool. Cube. Add onion, pepper, vinegar, boiled eggs, and a bit of salt. Allow to stand a couple of hours before mealtime.

## Potato Dumplings

Glenn Cardwell,
Greenbrier, TN

"That is the best dish you've ever tasted."

6 medium Irish potatoes,
   diced
2 c. water
$^1/_2$ tsp salt

$^1/_4$ tsp pepper
$^1/_2$ stick butter or margarine
3 c. milk, approximately

Cook potatoes in 2 cups water, season with salt and pepper. Add butter and milk and bring to a rousing boil. Drop dumplings into boiling center of potato mixture as fast as can, cover and simmer 8–10 minutes.

**DUMPLINGS**

$^1/_2$ c. flour
5 Tbsp shortening

Milk

Cut shortening into flour until crumbly. Add enough milk until dough sticks together. Roll out dough and cut into narrow strips, then cut again into $^1/_2$-inch squares.

---

## 'Tater Dumplings

Beuna Winchester,
Bryson City, NC

"I wish I could make 'tater dumplings as good as Mama could. . . That was one good way to fix Irish potatoes."

Irish potatoes
Chives

Dumpling dough

Cut potatoes into chunks and cook in water until semi-tender. When done, leave the potatoes in the excess water, add chives, and drop the little dumplings down in that. To warm them over, pour in long white enamel pan and brown them with the potatoes in stove. These will last for two meals and still be real tasty.

---

## Potato Cakes

If there were any leftover mashed potatoes on the camp or boardinghouse tables, "you can bet there would be potato cakes the next meal," said Rollins. Simple to make, but delicious.

During the Depression, some people ate potato cake sandwiches for lunch.

Rollins Justice, in Duane Oliver, *Cooking on Hazel Creek*

2 c. mashed potatoes      1 onion, chopped finely

Add onion to leftover mashed potatoes. Shape into round cakes and fry in a little fat from sausage or fatback pork. (A small amount of flour could be added to mixture to help them hold their shape.)

---

4 slices bacon
4 large potatoes, peeled and
    sliced thin

2 onions, peeled and sliced
1 c. water
Salt & pepper

## Mountain Fried Potatoes

Duane Oliver, *Cooking on Hazel Creek*

Fry bacon until crisp. Crumble and set aside. Fry potatoes and onions in drippings until lightly browned. Add salt, pepper, and bacon. Pour in enough water to almost cover the potatoes. Simmer 15 minutes or until tender. The water will cook away. When it does, turn potatoes over to brown and crisp.

"The first squash I can remember Mama growing (that wasn't in the form of a pumpkin) was these old white ones that look like a pie pan—they look like a little pie."

## Squash

Beuna Winchester, Bryson City, NC

Squash          Egg
Flour

Cut squashes in half, bake them, take the meat out of the inside, mix in flour and an egg, and make into patties and bake again. They can also be fried.

## Pumpkin

Beuna Winchester,
Bryson City, NC

*Pumpkin*        *Sugar*
*Butter*

Cut pumpkin into cubes and simmer in water until done. Season with butter and sugar, and eat like vegetable as would cooked sweet potatoes, except pumpkin is more watery.

## Fried Pumpkin

Duane Oliver,
*Cooking on Hazel Creek*

Everyone raised pumpkins on Hazel Creek, historian Duane Oliver writes. To keep them from freezing in winter, farmers buried the pumpkins under corn fodder in the barn loft. Pumpkins could also be dried by cutting into slices, running a stick through them, and hanging up. Rinds could be sliced off and reconstituted into stew, filling for pies, or as fried pumpkins.

Here is a nineteenth-century recipe for fried pumpkin:

*Pumpkin*        *Sugar*
*Salt*           *Cinnamon*

Cut pumpkin into cubes and simmer in water until done. Drain, mash the pumpkin, and place in skillet with a little salt and enough sugar to sweeten. Cinnamon can be added, if desired. Fry in bacon drippings for about 20 minutes.

## Turnip Greens with Cornmeal Dumplings

Edna Earley Welch,
in Duane Oliver,
*Cooking on Hazel Creek*

From Mrs. Welch's grandmother, who lived on Chambers Creek.

*3–4 lbs. turnip greens*      *1 1/2 c. boiling water*
*1 c. cornmeal*               *1/4 tsp salt*

Wash greens and add to boiling water. Cook until tender. In separate bowl, stir cornmeal into the 1 1/2 cups boiling water, add salt. Let cool. Drop by rounded tablespoon onto floured surface, roll into balls, flatten balls slightly. Drop dumplings into boiling greens, cover, reduce heat, and simmer 15 minutes.

"Good spring greens, they'll thin your blood."

**Poke Sallet**

Lucinda Ogle,
Gatlinburg, TN

Pick tender shoots of poke when it's first coming up. It's found along fences, fields, and roadsides. Pick until you have a mess, then wash thoroughly, boil a little bit the first time, pour off that water, boil again, pour that water off again, then run a little cold water over to wash it. Repeat boil once more, for total of three times, until water is clear. Fry greens in a skillet with grease.

2 lbs. young tender poke     2 eggs, slightly beaten
3 strips salt pork

**Poke
Greens**

Martha Whaley,
Gatlinburg, TN,
*Gatlinburg Recipe
Collection*

Cook poke in enough water to cover, about 20 minutes. Fry salt pork, add drained poke to grease, and fry about 5 minutes. Add eggs, cook until eggs are just set. Salt to taste. Serve with vinegar if desired.

Poke greens appear in late March in scrubby fields and along fencerows. Cut only the tender ones, 3 to 5 inches tall. Wash and look closely at each stalk. Boil at least three times in fresh water. Last time put greens into skillet into which bacon grease has been added. Salt lightly and heat thoroughly. Eat with cornbread.

**Poke
Greens**

Bonnie Myers,
Townsend, TN

## Fried Poke Stalks

Glenn Cardwell,
Greenbrier, TN

"These are the spring equivalent to the summer and fall fried okra, which is truly a good Southern dish. . . . If you love fried okra, you'll also enjoy fried poke stalks."

*Stalks of pokeweed*      *Cornmeal*
*Salted water*      *Bacon grease or oil*

Strip leaves from poke stalks. Slice stalks in shape of coins, soak in salt water 4–6 hours. Drain and rinse again. Drain well and roll pieces in cornmeal. Fry in bacon grease or oil in iron skillet, or put into oven until slightly brown. Salt and pepper to taste.

---

## Crowsfoot (Cut-leaved Toothwort)

Bonnie Myers,
Townsend, TN

This early wild green appears in mid March and into April, along creekbanks and small streams in the Smoky Mountains. Crowsfoot has a mustard flavor.

*Crowsfoot*      *Grease*
*Onion*

To prepare, wash crowsfoot. Place in bowl. Add cut up onion and almost hot pork grease. Fry and salt lightly.

---

## Ramps

Bonnie Myers,
Townsend, TN

The approach of spring in the mountains awakened folks' appetites for something new and green. Ramps grow at higher elevations in mountains, but harvesting is now prohibited in Great Smoky Mountains National Park.

*Ramps*      *Bacon grease*
*Salt*

To fix ramps, wash and remove filmy cover from bulbs. Cut leaves and bulbs into two-inch pieces. Salt lightly. Pour a small amount of warm bacon grease over them. Ramps go well with pinto beans and cornbread.

Peel the apples, cut out cores, and slice. Put in pan and just cover them with water. Cook real slow 'til they get soft, then sieve them or mash them up, add some sweetening and some spice to taste.

**Applesauce**

Mrs. Ollie Lawhern, *Maryville-Alcoa Times*

---

"An old Sheepnose apple made the prettiest bleached apple. Bleach with sulfur in a big wooden barrel."

Cut apples in quarters, layer them about six inches deep. A wire rack was hung over top of barrel near, but not touching, the apples. Put a spoonful of sulfur on piece of metal on rack in tin pan, and with long-handled tongs put sulphur on hot iron and lay in tin plate, cover quickly with old cloth or quilt. ("Don't let that sulfur smoke hit you in face.") Put in another layer of apples. Sulfured apples will keep all winter in that barrel and they'll stay snow white. Soak them to fix applesauce, apple pies or cakes, or canned apples.

**Sulfured (or Bleached) Apples**

Beuna Winchester, Bryson City, NC

**Dried Apples**

Beuna Winchester,
Bryson City, NC

Apples could be dried on a "dry kiln," which is like a sorghum furnace. Put a fire under it as do to make molasses, heat rocks under scaffold, and place fruit on top to dry. This kiln would hold three to four bushels of fresh apples, which would dry down to about a bushel. Dried apples are best to make stack cake.

---

**Fried Apples**

Lucinda Ogle,
Gatlinburg, TN

Core apples (use a tart apple like Summer Champion), don't peel them, fry in bacon fat until they're coated, then add a lot of sugar.

---

**Fried Apples**

Glenn Cardwell,
Greenbrier, TN

"If corn was the staff of life for the mountaineers, then apples were the spice of life."

*Four apples, (sweeter ones     Oil
such as Delicious,     $^1/_2$ stick butter
Limbertwig, Jonathan,     $^3/_4$ c. sugar
or McIntosh)*

Wash and quarter apples. Remove core and slice quarters thinly. Fry in oil until brown, stirring as needed to coat and brown sufficiently. Add butter and sugar and continue cooking until melted. Sweeter apples stay in chunkier pieces when fried; they do not cook up as much as tart apples do.

Mr. Justice noted that rhubarb was among the earliest things to grow in the garden in spring. "Like the wild greens, it was eagerly awaited for the first fresh pie, or the sauce or the spiced rhubarb. Besides being delicious on hot biscuits, it was considered a spring tonic."

**Spiced Rhubarb**

Rollins Justice, in Duane Oliver, *Cooking on Hazel Creek*

2 c. rhubarb, sliced          $^1/_4$ tsp allspice
2 c. sugar                    $^1/_4$ tsp ginger
$^1/_2$ tsp cinnamon          $^1/_4$ tsp nutmeg
$^1/_4$ tsp cloves

Cook cut rhubarb until tender. Add the sugar and any combination of spices listed that have on hand. Continue to cook, stirring often until thick.

# CORNBREAD
# & BISCUITS

## OF THE SMOKIES

# CORNBREAD & BISCUITS

"Give us this day our daily bread. . . ."
—The Lord's Prayer

Upon their arrival in the Great Smoky Mountains, European settlers were greeted by an unfamiliar sound echoing through the dense, green forest. It was the pounding of the Cherokee *ka no na*, a huge mortar and pestle consisting of a hollow log and a long pestle carved out of wood.

**Mollie Running Wolf pounding corn.**

With these devices, Cherokee women ground corn into meal, which they mixed with beans to make bean bread, *Tsu-Ya-Ga Du*. This traditional bread is still served at Cherokee get-togethers and in at least one restaurant in the busy tourist town of Cherokee, North Carolina, on the southern border of the park. Aggie Ross Lossiah, granddaughter of John Ross, principal chief of the Cherokees in the 1830s, told how to make bean bread. She prepared shelled corn as for hominy. Then she beat the corn in a *ka no na*, added cooked beans, formed the mixture into a flat ball, wrapped each ball in a husk of corn, and boiled them. She called these broadswords, similar to a Mexican tamale. No salt should be added, she advised, or bean bread would crumble.

To grind the corn and wheat they grew on their farms, Europeans introduced gristmills to the mountains. With abundant sources of flowing water for power, mills both small and large were located on streams throughout the Smokies. The basic principle involved pouring grain down onto two large round stones, called burrstones, with sharp beveled edges. The top, or runner stone, turned while the bottom, or bed, stone stayed stationary. The space between the rocks determined the coarseness or fineness of the meal. If the stones were dull or set too close together, the meal would scorch or burn.

A miller listened carefully to the sounds of the stones and felt the texture and temperature of the soft, warm meal pouring into the waiting bin. Said one miller, the work is "70 percent sound, 30 percent feel. . . . A blind man could run a mill." The rhythmic slow grinding could put a miller to sleep as surely as a lullaby. The smooth skin on the miller's thumb, it was said, was due to rubbing the meal between thumb and forefinger to check the consistency.

Burrstones were often imported from Europe, as Dr. John Mingus did for his mill on Mingus Creek near Oconaluftee. The Mingus family first built a mill of the classic overshot wheel style, like the Cable Mill that still runs in Cades Cove. Then, in 1886, Dr. Mingus hired Sion T. Early to build the mill Smokies visitors see today. Outside the three-story building, water from Mingus Creek runs through a millrace and oak flume into the penstock of a turbine situated beneath the mill. The turbine powers the stones.

Mingus Mill ground corn into meal and wheat into flour. In the second story of the mill, the wheat was cleaned, ground, then passed through the bolting chest, in essence a giant sifter that separated grades of fine flour, middlings, shorts, and bran. Mill day was a community event in the mountains. People loaded sacks of corn and wheat onto wagons or horses, made the journey to the mill and, while waiting for their "turn," spent the time visiting with others doing the same. Milling was a barter arrangement. In payment for his labor, a miller took a toll, usually an eighth of whatever amount of grain was to be ground.

Lovely wooden toll dishes were used for this purpose. While Mingus was a custom mill, grinding corn and flour to customers' specifications, smaller tub mills were scattered up and down the creeks near mountain homes. There were fourteen tub mills on Le Conte Creek alone. Noah "Bud" Ogle had a tub mill near his cabin, as did Alfred Reagan at the homeplace up on Roaring Fork.

Tub mills were so called because the waterwheel, made of soft wood such as pine or tuliptree, was enclosed in a wooden, tublike casing. (In the Smokies, however, no tub mills have been found that were so enclosed, but the name still applied.) Construction of the wheel and tub was an art in itself, one that has largely vanished from the southern mountains. The style dated to ancient Greek and Roman times. With its own tub mill, a family could enjoy fresh-ground meal anytime, without having to pay a toll; and, others from the neighborhood could come and have their corn ground too.

Fresh, stone-ground cornmeal—the only cornmeal as far as mountain people are concerned—can be bolted or unbolted. Unbolted is the whole, ground kernel, unsifted. Bolted cornmeal is sifted, removing the germ along with the rich corn flavor. Most mountain people prefer their cornmeal unbolted, and from white corn, of course.

While there were some yeast breads, the breads of choice among mountaineers were hot cornbread and biscuits, set on the table at breakfast, dinner, and supper. A host of different breads were made with cornmeal: cornpone, johnny cake, hoecake, ash cake, cornbread, gritted bread, cracklin' bread, and spoonbread were a few. The name cornpone likely derived from an early Indian bread, *appone* or *suppone*. A pone was a golden cake of cornbread patted flat and, in old times, baked in a lidded dutch oven with coals from the fireplace.

Ash cake was about as simple as they come: cornmeal, salt, and water formed into a pone, perhaps covered with a cabbage leaf or piece of cloth, and buried in ashes on the hearth. Hoecake was just what the name implies, a pone of cornbread baked on a clean hoe over a fire right in the field where people were working. If a hoe wasn't handy, a shovel would do.

Spoonbread is a dish still served with pride in many southern homes. Although recipes vary slightly, this moist bread centers on cornmeal with boiling water, eggs, butter, and milk. Some recipes call for separating the eggs, and include baking powder and sugar. Spoonbread is like a souffle, and when done is to be served with a spoon.

Country cornbread, hot from the oven with a fresh, nutty taste, was fundamental fare for Smokies folks. Earlier versions did not include flour, and some purists still scorn its use in cornbread. But as flour became cheaper and easier to come by, it was incorporated, making a cakier bread and tempering the unadulterated corn taste. Some people also insist true cornbread must contain buttermilk, while others are happy to use regular "sweet" milk.

Gritted bread was a seasonal specialty. In October, when corn was past the roasting ear stage but still milky sweet, it was time to make gritted bread. The name comes from the fact that corn was grated, or "gritted," on a tin grater, preferably homemade rather than store-bought. Sidney Saylor Farr gives specific directions for making a "gritter" in her cookbook, *More Than Moonshine*:

> Open a tin bucket at the seams and flatten it out until there is a piece approximately six or eight inches wide and sixteen to twenty inches long. Use a number 10 nail to punch holes at close intervals over the surface of the tin. Then cut a flat 1x6-inch board 24 inches long and nail two 1x21-inch strips lengthwise along the edges. Stretch the piece of tin, smooth side down, across and nail to each strip. This leaves a space between the tin and the board for the cornmeal to slide down in the pan.

The batter for gritted bread was poured into a greased, hot iron skillet and baked in a hot oven.

Wheat was not as plentiful in the mountains as corn, consequently flour was a highly valued commodity. One of the greatest uses of flour was in making biscuits. If a family raised wheat and had flour, biscuits were everyday bread; otherwise, they were a special treat on Sundays.

"Mama had one of them big old Home Comfort stoves," reminisced Beuna Winchester, "and any time, any time during the day there would be . . . biscuits in that old warming closet up there." Her father grew wheat and had it ground into flour at a mill. They had "biscuit bread" for breakfast, biscuits and meat for dinner, and biscuits for school.

When flour had to be purchased, it was in fifty- or 100-pound bags brought home and stored in a "meal gum," a hollow log or wooden box that was a fixture in most mountain kitchens.

Alongside the meal or flour was kept a big wooden bread tray, or doughbowl, ready for a cook to stir up bread on a moment's notice. To make biscuits, she would put flour in the doughbowl; make a well, or indention, in the middle; pour in the milk and/ or water; and work in lard with her hands. Experts pinched off

The John Cable Mill ground both cornmeal and wheat flour. It continues to operate in Cades Cove today.
*1936 by E. E. Exline*

the exact amount of dough for each biscuit, each one consistently the same size. For those who preferred dough rolled out with a rolling pin, a biscuit cutter could be made by removing one end of tin can and punching holes in the other end. Biscuits were baked quickly in a hot oven, until puffy and golden brown.

Before leavening products were available, a bread called beaten biscuits was leavened by sheer muscle power. A firm dough of flour, lard, and milk was beaten with a mallet or other heavy object, then folded and kneaded for about half an hour. A book of recipes from the year 1776 gave these instructions for making beaten biscuits: "Place on a smooth flat surface of a tree stump and beat with an iron pestle or side of a hatchet until the dough raises little blisters of air and is smooth and satiny."

In parts of the South, beaten biscuits were something of a status symbol; having them meant the homeowner kept slaves, who actually did the hard work. In 1877, a hand-cranked kneading machine was patented to lessen the labor, which helped somewhat. But only in the upper South did beaten biscuits retain their popularity. John Egerton, historian of southern food, says that's because this is the country ham belt, and "Southerners who could resist paper-thin slices of prime country ham piled high between halves of a beaten biscuit were few and far between. They still are."

Cooks must have been overjoyed with the availability of baking soda around 1840, followed by the introduction of baking powder in 1856. The lightest, fluffiest biscuits were leavened with baking powder, which contains baking soda, cream of tartar, and cornstarch or flour. For the liquid, buttermilk was used; its acidity enhanced the power of the leavening agent and resulted in a tender, soft crumb. Richer biscuits were made with cream or even whipping cream. Some were so heavenly they earned the name "angel biscuits."

The flour often favored for biscuits was made by the White Lily company in Knoxville, Tennessee. This mill, still operating after 115 years, produces an all-purpose flour from soft winter wheat. Soft wheat is lower in protein than hard wheat, which means less gluten, the substance that gives elasticity to bread dough. For tender biscuits, cakes, and flaky piecrusts, though, gluten was not desirable. So White Lily, with the consistency of cake flour, remains the flour of choice among mountain biscuit makers.

White Lily also makes a self-rising flour, which contains the baking powder, salt, and soda. Self-rising flour was designed to make biscuitry a surer, quicker art. As with baking powder, though, self-rising flour had to be used when fresh or results could be disappointing. The importance of a cook's ability to bake a good biscuit could hardly be overstated. Some cooks eschewed such shortcuts, sticking to the tried-and-true "pinch of this and dab of that" proportions their grannies taught them.

Leftover biscuits were sometimes transformed into a sweet

*"Two hundred licks is what I gives For home-folks, never fewer, An' if I'm 'specting company in, I gives five hundred sure!"*

dish. The biscuits were layered with berries and sugar and set out overnight for "cold pie," perfectly permissible for breakfast the next morning. If a person didn't want to take time to make biscuits, a faster version called flitter bread—a crispy thin biscuit dough baked in a pan—could be stirred together. And Horace Kephart, over in North Carolina, told of "lath-open" bread, prepared like regular biscuit dough with soda and buttermilk but with the shortening worked in at the end. Baked as flat cakes, this bread had "the peculiar property of parting readily into thin flakes when broken edgewise."

The word "biscuit" rarely appears without the word "gravy." The simplest was clear, red-eye gravy made from the residue of cooked ham, with water or coffee added. "Split big biscuits, spoon the gravy over them, take a slice of ham . . . that's eat'n," opined one mountaineer. The other form was a white gravy made with milk or cream, thickened with flour, with hefty chunks of sausage suspended in it. This gravy, poured over a plate of biscuits, was guaranteed to fill an empty hole in a person's stomach.

White gravy with cornmeal as the thickener was called sawmill gravy. Lucinda Ogle told a story of how sawmill gravy originated. One day, way back in the woods at the logging camp at Tremont, the cooks ran out of flour. They didn't know what in the world to do, so they made the gravy out of cornmeal. The new workers who came in the next morning asked, "What kind of gravy have you got today?"

"We made it out of sawdust," the cooks replied.

(As an interesting historical note, by 1912 in stores near the logging camp of Elkmont, cornmeal sold for 50 cents a bushel and white flour was 50 cents for 50 pounds. Entire families went with the menfolk to live in bunkhouses at the camps. Before the men set off to work each day, they ate a huge breakfast of big cat-head biscuits with jelly, honey, or molasses; platters of sausage or side meat; brook trout; eggs; and plenty of strong coffee. They needed these hearty breakfasts, for they worked seven days a week, hauling timber for six days then cutting wood for the skidder on Sundays.)

It is no exaggeration to say that a few people today are obsessed with biscuits. A man named Stephen Harrigan confessed to such a life-long obsession, tracing it to a biscuit he ate around 1955 at his grandmother's house in Tennessee. "My grandmother," Harrigan wrote, "died before I had the sense to ask her for the recipe, and so for these many years I have trod the earth, looking for a biscuit that could recapture for me that primal moment."

He might want to try one of the recipes here.

**Bean Bread**
*Tsu-Ya-Ga*

Aggie Ross
Lossiah,
*Cherokee Cooklore*

This is the way Aggie Lossiah made bean bread, a classic Cherokee food. It is the way her "old Cherokee granny made it" when they lived in a cave on the Tennessee River, before grist mills came with the white settlers.

Put beans on to cook separately in a pot. Cook flour corn in kettle of wood ash lye water, stirring until skin slips off. Wash corn in basket sieve to remove skins. Beat corn in wooden beater until fine. Pour hot beans and their soup into pan of meal. Do not add salt, or bean bread will crumble. Work quickly while mixture is still warm, and pat into balls. You can cook them like this, or flatten into dumplings, called broadswords, and wrap each in a blade of corn. Fold ends under or tie with a strong grass. Drop into boiling water, cook for about an hour. Eat plain, with butter, meat grease, wild game, "as suits one's fancy."

**Cornbread Baked on Bark**

Aggie Ross
Lossiah,
Cherokee, NC,
*Cherokee Cooklore*

When traveling, the Cherokees were not able to carry their cooking utensils with them so they had to improvise. When it was time to cook bread, one of the men would carefully cut pieces of bark from a chestnut tree. The dough was put on the inside of the bark and this was stood up before the fire to cook. The combination of bark, woodsmoke, and hunger made this bread about the best any Indian ever ate.

**Ash Cakes**

Aggie Ross
Lossiah,
Cherokee, NC

Mix cornmeal and warm water into a stiff dough. Rake ashes back from the hot stone at the bottom of fireplace and cover with oak leaves. Place the cornpone on the leaves and cover all with red-hot ashes. Remove pone when done.

This recipe came from a 108-year-old East Tennessee woman! Ash cake may have been passed to European settlers by Cherokees.

## Ash Cake

Sidney Saylor Farr, *More Than Moonshine*

| | |
|---|---|
| *1 tsp salt* | *Boiling water* |
| *1 quart sifted cornmeal* | |

Stir salt with cornmeal. Pour into mixture enough boiling water to make a thick mush. Shape dough into round, flat cakes. Sweep a clean place on the hottest part of the hearth. Put cakes on this spot and cover with hot wood ashes. When bread is done, wash and wipe dry. But if you wrap each cake in a cabbage leaf before covering with ashes, you will not need to wash cakes before eating them.

---

Beat cornmeal as for other types of bread. Make dumplings rather thin, boil in plain water until done. Let cool, split open, and spread in flat basket. This basket of split dumplings was passed over the flame four times, once each to the North, East, South, and West, to keep the Skillies off. Then the basket was set outside to freeze, and the bread was eaten in the morning while still frozen. The smoke left a very pleasant flavor to the bread. Old people especially got lots of pleasure from sitting by a good fire on an icy day, slowly munching on a bit of frozen bread while telling younger ones about the olden days.

## Flat Dumplings

Aggie Ross Lossiah, Cherokee, NC, *Cherokee Cooklore*

---

| | |
|---|---|
| *2 c. self-rising cornmeal* | *1 egg* |
| *¹/2 c. chopped green onions,* | |
| *tops included* | |

## Hoecake

Dick Whaley, Gatlinburg, TN, *Gatlinburg Recipe Collection*

Mix all ingredients together and add milk to make soft dough. Dip with tablespoon into hot skillet with shortening or oil ¹/2-inch deep. Fry on both sides until brown. Serve hot.

## Hoecake, another version

Sidney Saylor Farr,
*More Than Moonshine*

Traditionally, pones of hoecake were baked on a clean hoe over a fire, hence the name.

| | |
|---|---|
| *4 c. cornmeal* | *1 Tbsp bacon drippings* |
| *Boiling water* | *1 tsp salt* |

Preheat oven to 425 degrees. Scald cornmeal with enough boiling water to make a stiff dough. Add bacon drippings and salt, stirring well. Shape into oval pones, one handful of dough at a time, and put in a greased pan. (Mother and Granny always left the imprints of their fingers across the tops.) Bake in hot oven until brown. These hoecakes may also be baked in a skillet on top of the stove, turning each pone once to brown both sides.

---

## Johnny-Cakes

Sidney Saylor Farr,
*More Than Moonshine*

Johnny-cakes were made by Mrs. Farr's Granny Brock, who told her she supposed the name for this bread came from the time when a pioneer woman was fixing her hungry little boy a cake of cornbread that would be "Johnny's cake." Other versions say it was bread suitable to be carried on a journey, and the "johnny" is a corruption of the word "journey."

| | |
|---|---|
| *$^1/_2$ c. flour* | *1 egg, beaten lightly* |
| *1 c. cornmeal* | *1 c. hot water or milk* |
| *1 tsp sugar* | *1 Tbsp shortening* |
| *1 tsp salt* | |

Mix the dry ingredients, then stir in the rest. Drop or pour on hot, greased griddle or iron skillet and fry to a golden brown on both sides. Serve with butter as a bread or with molasses as pancakes. Makes 4 to 6 servings.

This is a basic, nineteenth-century cornbread recipe, made in a dutch oven on the fireplace.

**Cornbread**

Duane Oliver,
Cooking on Hazel
Creek

2 c. cornmeal
2 tsp baking powder
1 tsp soda
1 tsp salt

1 egg, beaten
2 c. buttermilk
1/4 c. melted fat

Combine dry ingredients, then add egg, milk, and fat. Stir until moistened, but do not beat. Pour into greased dutch oven, put lid on and set in coals by fireplace, heaping coals on the lid. Bake for about a half hour. When done, carefully remove lid so top will brown and some of the steam will escape. (A few ashes may get on the bread when the lid is removed, but they're good for you because they're full of potassium.)

(Printed on back of bag of stone-ground cornmeal, sold by Great Smoky Mountains Association.)

**Cornbread**

1 1/2 c. sour milk or buttermilk
2 eggs
1 Tbsp sugar
1/2 tsp salt
1/2 tsp baking soda

1 1/2 c. cornmeal
1/2 c. flour
1/4 c. melted butter or
    margarine

Beat the first five ingredients together. Stir in the cornmeal and flour. Add melted butter. Mix. Pour batter into a greased, 8 inch square pan. Bake at 425 degrees for 30 minutes or until golden brown.

## Steamed Corn Pone

Adele (Mrs. Boyd) McKenzie, *Sam Houston Schoolhouse Cookbook*

This is pone the way her grandmothers, Mrs. S. A. Patton and Mrs. I. A. Broady, made it.

| | |
|---|---|
| 3 c. plain cornmeal | 1 tsp salt |
| 1 c. flour | $^1/_2$ tsp baking powder |
| 1 tsp soda | |

Combine and add:

| | |
|---|---|
| 1 egg | $^1/_2$ c. cooking oil |
| 2 c. sweet (whole) milk | $^1/_2$ c. molasses |

Sift flour, soda, salt, and baking powder and add to cornmeal. Stir in egg, milk, oil, and molasses. Pour into greased and lined small tube pan or 4 cans (ca. 202 size). Place over hot water, being careful to keep water out of bread. Cover and steam slowly 2$^1/_2$ hours. Remove from pan or can. Place in hot oven to dry. Loaves can be frozen and reheated. The Broadys served with fried chicken, the Pattons with boiled dinners, such as beans or cabbage.

---

## Spoonbread

Mildred Bunting, Blowing Rock, NC, *Gatlinburg Recipe Collection*

| | |
|---|---|
| 2$^1/_2$ c. boiling water | 1 tsp baking powder |
| 2 c. cornmeal | 1 tsp salt |
| 2 egg yolks | 3 Tbsp melted butter |
| 2 egg whites, stiffly beaten | 1$^1/_2$ c. buttermilk |

Stir cornmeal gradually into boiling water; let cool. Add beaten egg yolks, baking powder, and salt, also add melted butter and the buttermilk. Fold in stiffly beaten egg whites. Bake in greased baking dish at 425 degrees for 45 minutes. Serves 8.

---

## Spoonbread

Whitley J. Potter, Gatlinburg, TN, *Gatlinburg Recipe Collection*

| | |
|---|---|
| 1 pint milk (heat to boiling point) | 2 Tbsp melted fat |
| $^1/_2$ c. cornmeal | 1 tsp salt |
| $^1/_2$ tsp baking powder | 3 egg yolks |
| | 3 egg whites, stiffly beaten |

Stir cornmeal gradually into heated milk and cook in double boiler until consistency of mush. Add baking powder, salt, fat, and egg yolks. Fold in stiffly beaten egg whites. Pour into a hot greased baking dish and bake at 375 degrees for 30 minutes. Serves 6.

---

### Southern Spoonbread

Annette Hartigan, Knoxville, TN

1 pint buttermilk
1 c. cornmeal (unbolted)
1 tsp salt
1 tsp soda

*1/2 c. sweet whole milk*
*3 eggs (beat yolks and whites separately)*

Preheat oven to 350 degrees. Mix dry ingredients together, then add milk and egg yolk and mix until there are no lumps of corn-meal. Then fold in *stiffly* beaten egg whites. Pour into a 1¹/₂-quart casserole and cover top with pats of butter. Bake 35–40 minutes. Test for doneness by shaking gently. If the center moves, bake a little longer, until firm and light golden brown. Serve hot with butter. Serve with a spoon.

---

### Great Smokies Spoonbread

(On back of bag of stone-ground cornmeal, sold by Great Smoky Mountains Association)

1 c. cornmeal
2 c. cold water
2 tsp salt

1 c. milk
2 or 3 eggs
2 Tbsp fat

Mix meal, water, and salt. Boil 5 minutes, stirring. Add milk, well-beaten eggs, and fat. Mix well. Pour into well-greased hot pan or baking dish. Bake 50 minutes at 375 degrees. Serve from the dish.

## Gritted Bread

Beuna Winchester,
Bryson City, NC

Use field or flour corn, a little riper and firmer than roasting ear stage. Remove husks and silks from about a dozen ears. Grate (or "grit") kernels off cobs with coarse grater, deep into the cob to get corn "milk." Cooked green beans may also be added. Pour corn into greased baking pan and bake at 350 degrees about 45 minutes.

---

## Gritted Bread

Mollie
Runningwolfe
Sequoyah,
Cherokee, NC,
*Cherokee Cooklore*

Pull corn that is just a little too hard for roasting ears. Grit this corn on a homemade gritter. Make into bean bread or just plain bread. If the plain bread was baked real done, it would last a week in any weather without souring. This kind of bread could be baked in the woods by spreading leaves of cucumber tree on a clean spot of ground or on a stone. To cook it this way, put the dough on the leaves and cover with more leaves, then cover the whole thing with live coals and hot ashes. Let cook until done.

## Cracklin' Bread

Sidney Saylor Farr,
*More Than
Moonshine*

Cracklin's are the crispy brown residue left in bottom of kettle in which lard is made. They are mixed into this simple cornbread recipe.

2 c. cornmeal
1 tsp salt
2 tsp baking powder

2 c. cracklin's, cut in small
pieces
Boiling water

Sift together cornmeal, salt, and baking powder. Mix in cracklins' and enough boiling water to make medium dough. Heat a greased iron skillet, sprinkle with flour, and pour in dough. Bake at 400 to 450 degrees until brown. Serve hot. A richer cornbread can be made with eggs and buttermilk.

---

Crumble leftover cornbread, fry until crisp and brown in grease in skillet. Eat with sweet milk.

### Poor Do

Lucinda Ogle,
Gatlinburg, TN

---

This is an old-time version of dressing, or stuffing, to be served with poultry.

### Cush

Mrs. Reva Hurst,
Sevierville, TN,
*Homespun Recipes*

| | |
|---|---|
| 2 Tbsp bacon drippings | $^1/_2$ c. chopped onion |
| 2 Tbsp margarine | 2 eggs |
| 3 c. cornbread and biscuits | Milk |
| 1 $^1/_2$ tsp ground sage | Salt & pepper to taste |

Heat bacon drippings and margarine in heavy skillet. Break up old cornbread and biscuits (use more cornbread than biscuits). Add to hot fat, along with salt, pepper, sage, onion, and eggs. Stir and brown lightly. Then add milk to make soft batter and cook until fairly dry. Or bake at 350 degrees for 25–30 minutes.

---

| | |
|---|---|
| 5 c. flour | 1 c. shortening |
| 4 Tbsp sugar | 1 cake yeast dissolved in |
| 1 tsp salt | tablespoon lukewarm water |
| 3 Tbsp baking powder | 2 c. buttermilk |
| 1 tsp soda | |

### Angel Biscuits

Mrs. Manker Inman,
Sevierville, TN,
*Homespun Recipes*,
with Lucinda Ogle,
Gatlinburg, TN

Sift dry ingredients together and cut in shortening. Then add buttermilk and yeast mixture. Knead well. Roll out dough, cut with big biscuit cutter, brush with melted margarine, fold over, put on baking sheet with a little space between each one. Let rise in warm place. Dough can be used immediately or kept in refrigerator for several days. Bake at 375–400 degrees for 12–15 minutes.

---

**Buttermilk Biscuits**

Mary Ruble,
*Reminiscing With Recipes*

| | |
|---|---|
| 2 c. flour | $^1/_3$ tsp soda |
| 1 tsp baking powder | 4 Tbsp fat |
| $^3/_4$ tsp salt | $^2/_3$ c. buttermilk |

Mix dry ingredients. Cut in fat with two knives, then add the milk. Knead slightly, roll and cut. Bake in hot oven (450–500 degrees).

---

**Buttermilk Biscuits**

Mrs. Ollie Lawhern,
*Maryville-Alcoa Times*

| | |
|---|---|
| 2 c. sifted flour | $^1/_2$ tsp baking soda |
| $^3/_4$ tsp salt | 5 Tbsp shortening |
| 2 tsp baking powder | Buttermilk to make soft dough |

Sift flour, salt, baking powder, and soda together. Cut in shortening until mixture looks like cornmeal. Mix in buttermilk. Turn out onto lightly floured board, flour hands and knead dough "easy like" 10–15 times. Roll out or pat out until about $^3/_8$-inch thick. Cut round with an old baking powder can. Put in ungreased pan and bake in a hot oven (450 degrees) 12–15 minutes or until tops are golden brown. Serve hot with lots of butter, molasses, or honey.

---

**Cabin Buttermilk Biscuits**

Beuna Winchester,
Bryson City, NC

| | |
|---|---|
| 2 c. flour | 2 tsp baking powder |
| $^1/_4$ tsp baking soda | 5 Tbsp shortening |
| 1 tsp salt | 1 c. buttermilk |

Sift dry ingredients together and blend with lard or shortening. Add buttermilk, about one cup to make soft dough. Roll out to

$^1/_4$- to $^1/_2$-inch thick, cut with biscuit cutter. Place on baking sheet and bake in 350-degree oven (in woodstove) about 10 minutes, or until brown. For modern gas or electric stove, bake at 475–500 degrees.

---

Stir up like biscuit bread in previous recipe, but make a thin dough, pour it in a pan, and bake it. It will be real crispy. Flitter bread was made if you didn't want to take time to make biscuits.

### Flitter Bread

Beuna Winchester,
Bryson City, NC

---

To make big cat-head biscuits, use the aforementioned Cabin Buttermilk Biscuits ingredients. But, instead of rolling out dough, keep it in a big loaf. For each biscuit, pinch off a piece of dough about the size of a big lemon and pat it out with your hands. For more than a hundred years, mountain men have said big cat-head biscuits were their favorite biscuits when drowned in sawmill gravy.

### Cat-Head Biscuits

Beuna Winchester,
Bryson City, NC

---

2 c. self-rising flour          1 c. whipping cream
2 tsp sugar

Combine all ingredients and blend well. Dough will be stiff. Knead, roll $^3/_8$ inch thick. Cut. Place on greased pan. Bake at 450 degrees 10–12 minutes.

### Whipping Cream Biscuits

Uneta Allen
Potter, from her
grandmother, Sarah
Wood Allen, and
her aunt, Molly
Lail,
*Sam Houston
Schoolhouse
Cookbook*

## Chestnut Bread

Beuna Winchester,
Bryson City, NC

*2 lbs. chestnuts, shelled and broken into bits*
*8 c. plain cornmeal*

*3 Tbsp baking powder*
*3 Tbsp baking soda*

Boil the shelled chestnuts 10–15 minutes in a half gallon of hot water. Add sugar to taste. Pour this boiling liquid into the cornmeal mixture and stir well. Add enough hot water to make a stiff dough. Form this into round dumplings. Wrap each dumpling in blade from green corn, tuck in loose ends. Drop dumplings into a big pot of boiling water. Cook an hour or more. When they sink to bottom, they're done. Best served hot, some like them with butter.

---

## Fried Bread

Beuna Winchester,
Bryson City, NC

*2 c. flour*
*2 Tbsp baking powder*
*1 tsp salt*

*1 c. milk*
*2 lbs. shortening*

Sift dry ingredients together. Add milk to make soft dough. Roll like biscuits and cut into squares, making a slit in each square. Heat shortening and drop in squares of bread dough. Brown on each side.

---

## Cornmeal Dumplings

Glenn Cardwell,
Greenbrier, TN

**BROTH**

Cook hambone in water for about an hour or two, leave a lot of ham on bone; when cooked, remove bone from liquid. "Give bone to that old blue-tick hound."

**DUMPLINGS**

*2 c. self-rising cornmeal*
*(If unbolted, use 4 c. of meal and add baking soda and baking powder)*

*Milk or water*
*Salt and pepper to taste*

Mix cornmeal with enough water or milk for dough to stick

together. Taste broth to make sure it's not already too salty. Spoon dumpling dough into boiling broth, cook covered 8–10 minutes.

---

Pawpaws are also called mountain bananas, because their taste resembles that fruit. They have been called the "perfect food" by nutritionists, and modern agricultural researchers have been trying to encourage farmers to grow pawpaws as a high-value crop.

**Pawpaw Bread**

Sidney Saylor Farr, *More Than Moonshine*

| | |
|---|---|
| 2 c. sifted all-purpose flour | 1 c. pawpaw pulp (from about 6 |
| 1 tsp soda | peeled and seeded pawpaws) |
| 1/2 tsp salt | 1/3 c. milk |
| 1/2 c. butter | 1 tsp lemon juice |
| 1 c. sugar | 1/2 c. chopped nuts (at least |
| 2 eggs | 1/3 should be black walnuts) |

Preheat oven to 350 degrees. Sift flour with soda and salt. Cream butter. Gradually add sugar, creaming well after each addition. Stir in eggs and pawpaw pulp; blend thoroughly. Combine milk and lemon juice and alternately add dry and liquid ingredients to pawpaw mixture, beginning and ending with dry ingredients. Stir in nuts. Grease bottom of 9x5x3-inch pan. Pour in batter. Bake for 60–70 minutes or until bread springs back when lightly touched in the center. Remove from pan, cool on rack.

---

| | |
|---|---|
| Bacon drippings or ham | Milk |
| grease | Salt & pepper |
| 2–3 Tbsp flour | Water |

**Sawmill Gravy**

Beuna Winchester, Bryson City, NC

Use grease left in skillet after frying meat. Remove the meat, add the flour to the hot grease, let it brown slightly. Thin the mixture a little with water, then add milk and salt and pepper. Stir and cook until fairly thick.

## Sawmill Gravy

Nancy Cooper,
Gatlinburg, TN,
*Gatlinburg Recipe Collection*

*1 lb. sausage*
*2 Tbsp flour (or more)*
*1 1/2 c. milk*

*Water*
*Salt and pepper*

Make sausage into patties and fry in moderately hot skillet until brown and cooked done. Drain sausage patties on paper towels. Use about half of grease in skillet to make gravy. Brown the flour in the grease, stirring constantly. Add milk and enough water to make gravy as thin as you like. Break up about four of the cooked sausage patties and crumble in the gravy. Salt and pepper to taste. Serve over hot biscuits.

---

## Sawmill Gravy

Lucinda Ogle,
Gatlinburg, TN

*Bacon*
*1/2 c. cornmeal*

*Sweet (whole) milk*

To make her sawmill gravy, Lucinda fries bacon, adds cornmeal to the grease in pan, then stirs constantly until brown; watch so it doesn't scorch. Add sweet milk, enough to make gravy the consistency you like. If too thick, add more milk.

---

## Glenn's Gravy

Glenn Cardwell,
Greenbrier, TN

"Before God drove Adam and Eve out of the Garden of Eden, he gave Eve the recipe for gravy and it's been in the family ever since." For Sunday brunch, Glenn makes the gravy while his wife, Faye, makes biscuits. Glenn fries the potatoes and eggs.

*Sausage*
*3 Tbsp self-rising flour*

*Milk*
*Salt and pepper to taste*

In an iron skillet, get a base of frying sausage (or bacon). After done frying, there are a lot of good sediments left in the skillet. Leave 2 tablespoons of grease in the skillet, stir in 3 tablespoons of self-rising flour into grease, and brown it. "The secret of good gravy is to brown that flour slowly," says Glenn.

Stir in milk, usually about 3 cups, or until gravy is desired consistency. Salt and pepper to taste.

Meat (optional)
Water or milk
Salt

Red pepper
Cornmeal

## Cornmeal Gravy

Jim Will,
Cherokee, NC,
*Cherokee Cooklore*

Put some water, or milk if have it, salt, and red pepper in a skillet in which meat has been cooked. If you don't have meat, just put the ingredients in a clean skillet. Add cornmeal and cook until meal is done. Eat by itself or with bread for breakfast or with vegetables.

# SWEETENINGS
# & DESSERTS

### O F   T H E   S M O K I E S

# SWEETENINGS & DESSERTS
## (CAKES, PIES, COBBLERS, COOKIES, AND CANDY)

"Most honey is made by bees. But sourwood is made by bees and angels."                                    —Carson Brewer

A strong sweet tooth runs through the ranks of mountain people. Desserts and sweets brightened up meals and were served in honor of most holidays and special occasions. But for the early settlers, sugar was expensive and sometimes difficult to obtain. So they did what they've always done and looked to the goodness of natural sources for sweetening.

First they went to the sugar maple trees. Lucinda Ogle remembers making lollipops in the early 1900s, when she was a very small child. Her Grandpappy Oakley had a good stand of big sugar maples in his yard. On days in early spring, when the sap was rising and snow was still on the ground, he tapped the trees and boiled the sap to make maple syrup. While he did that, he'd send Lucinda and her sisters and brothers out to gather birch twigs and pans of snow. Then Grandpa Oakley poured thick ribbons of syrup across the snow, and the children put the twigs into the syrup as it cooled to form the "suckers."

*Use pine wood when boiling molasses, and it will not be sticky or smoky.*

Maple trees were also tapped in the "sugar orchard" in Greenbrier Cove above the Fittified Spring (one that flowed fitfully). Glenn Cardwell, who grew up in the Greenbrier area, remembered older folk saying that in springtime "it'd come a warm wind over that mountain and the maple sap would start flowing." The logs of the linn, or white basswood tree, were used as troughs for collecting the syrup. By the 1920s, however, most of the large, valuable sugar maple trees in the Smokies had been cut down by timber companies, and maple sugar making came to an end in most parts of the mountains.

Another dark, sticky syrup was made from the juice of a cane plant called sorghum. Sorghum molasses is made from sorghum cane, which resembles the corn plant but with narrower leaves and no ears. Most mountain farms had a cane patch. Seeds were planted in spring, and some farmers held that sorghum cane planted in dark ground produced dark sorghum molasses, while that planted in light ground yielded light syrup. When the seed heads turned red and hard, it was time to harvest the cane. This needed to be done before the first frost, usually by late September or early October.

Harvesting sorghum cane. *circa 1930 by Carlos Campbell*

The plants' leaves and seed heads were stripped, and the cane was cut. It was taken without delay to a sorghum mill. Because molasses-making was something of a specialty, usually only a few people in any area had a mill, people with names like "Sugar John."

On molasses-making day, a horse or mule was hitched up to a long rein pole, or sweep. As the animal walked around in a circle, it powered crusher rollers in the mill. Someone would feed the long stalks between the rollers, and the juice was squeezed out into a barrel.

After careful straining, the green juice was transferred to the cooker, or evaporator, where it was boiled for several hours

Squeezing cane with a horse-powered sorghum mill. *1959 by R. M. Schiele*

until it turned into the golden brown liquid so valued for sweetening. Molasses-making was a day-long process requiring several good hands for assistance. The sight of steam coming off the vat and the delectable scent of the cooking juice was a wonderful ritual of autumn in the mountains.

The evaporator was a fascinating device. A fire was built in the cooker, and a metal pan, often of copper, sat on top of the cooker. Evaporators often had four to as many as eight chambers. In the first compartment, the fresh juice was brought to a boil, stirred steadily, and released into the second compartment, where boiling continued. As the water evaporated and the juice thickened, it was then shifted into the third compartment, where the foam on the surface was skimmed off with a long-handled, perforated "skimmer."

**Boiling sorghum syrup down to molasses.**
*courtesy Carlos Campbell*

(The skimmings were often dumped into a hole, or sometimes corked in a jug and fermented for a punchy drink.)

Then the juice was passed into the final chamber where it cooked a little longer. With an expert eye, a master molasses maker could tell the crucial moment when the juice was ready to be "pulled" or drawn off. As the bubbles on the surface started to look the way jelly does when it's about done, the molasses was close. He might dip in a piece of fresh cane now and then for a taste, or let the juice drip from a wooden paddle to see when it made a thick, gold skein. When he judged the molasses ready, a plug was pulled and the hot, amber liquid filled waiting jars. If pulled off too soon, the molasses would separate or clabber. If too late, it would be exceedingly stiff, or worse, burned.

Knowing when molasses was done involved more art than science. "There ain't no set rule when it comes to makin' molasses," according to Arvel Greene. As he told author John Parris, "A clock don't do no good to go by. You just get a feelin' when they're ready, and you take 'em off."

Molasses-making is another one of those mountain skills that has nearly disappeared, and is now done mostly for the benefit of visiting tourists. An old-timer, seeing gleaming pure sorghum molasses, would give his soul for a jar or two. Sorghum was spread on biscuits and used as the sweetening in pies, cakes, cookies, and superior gingerbreads. At Christmastime, it was often made into a syrup candy. The syrup was boiled until thick and stiff in a heavy pot. It was poured out and separated into portions. People greased their hands and pulled and stretched the candy until the color became foamy yellow, like taffy.

The only other substance that shared the stage with sorghum molasses was honey. Sorghum was called "short sweetenin'" and honey was "long sweetenin'." In some ways honey was easier and cheaper to obtain than molasses because it didn't require growing a crop or a long preparation. What honey did require was a person brave enough to "course through the woods" after wild bees, locate the tree they were living in, and rob the hive.

*A swarm of bees in May is worth a ton of hay.*

*A swarm of bees in June is worth a silver spoon.*

*A swarm of bees in July is not worth a fly.*

During the Civil War, sugar was so scarce mountain people were forced to gather wild honey. In these extremely lean years, women made "cakes"

using this honey instead of sugar, and a batter without eggs, butter, or milk. As one writer said, "It was, indeed, cooking from scratch at a time when even scratch was hard to come by."

George Lemon and his bee hives.
*by E. E. Exline*

According to historian and author Wilma Dykeman, five years after the Civil War the Cataloochee section of the Smoky Mountains, in western North Carolina, produced some 2,000 pounds of honey and about 1,320 quarts of sorghum molasses. With cash or trade from that honey, parents could buy shoes, books, tablets, pencils and other supplies their children needed for school. And, into the twentieth century, author Horace Kephart reported that the local preacher "had a hundred hives of tame bees, producing 1,500 pounds of honey a year, for which he got ten cents a pound at the railroad."

Earl Ramsey of Seymour, Tennessee, comes from a long line of beekeepers. His grandfather was Harvey Oakley, whose homeplace was on Twin Creeks in the Smokies. In addition to seven different apple orchards, his grandpa also kept a large number of bees. Earl's father, James Isaac Ramsey, hunted bee trees and robbed them, and Earl has done the same. He and a friend found more than fifty bee trees in one season, "cut six or eight or ten of them," and caught the bees in burlap sacks. In

**Capitalizing on the early tourist trade.**
*by E. E. Exline*

catching a swarm, it was critical to get the queen so the hive continued to reproduce. According to Earl, the honeybees were Italian, English, Egyptian, and German strains brought in by settlers. The bees then swarmed and became wild. A swarm is caused when an older queen and most of the worker bees leave an overcrowded hive. If there is a younger queen, she stays in the old hive. Catching a swarm, then, allowed a beekeeper to add to his number of hives.

The standard, square, wooden beehive seen today was invented by a pastor in Pennsylvania in 1851. But observant mountaineers simply adapted what the bees were doing naturally. For many years past 1851, they had homemade beehives. These hives were nothing more than a hollow log, usually from a blackgum tree, and hence were called "beegums." Earl Ramsey told how a beegum was made: cut off about a thirty-inch section of the tree, set it over a hot fire to burn out the deadwood, bore holes and insert two crossed sticks, then put a lid on top. The cross sticks were the framework for the honeycomb. Small notches were cut into the base of the hive so the bees could come and go.

The best time to make a beegum was in fall and winter. A swarm of bees would be brought in and established in late March and early April, and the honey was harvested in August and September. The better honey was taken above the cross sticks,

said Earl, and what was below the cross sticks was left so the bees had something to feed on through the winter.

If Earl beat with a hammer to remove the lid, "the bees got real mad. A lot of keeping bees," he observed, "is how you handle them." They don't like sudden moves or noises. When Earl goes in to work his bees, he watches the weather and does not go on a cool morning or during a thunderstorm. The best time to work them is on a clear, sunny day.

Beekeepers must check on their hives occasionally to make

Steve Cole and his bees in the Sugarlands area of the Great Smoky Mountains.
*by E. E. Exline*

sure there are no problems. "Mice are bad to go in 'em in wintertime," Earl noted. They eat the comb for protein.

The quality and taste of any honey depends entirely on which plants bees forage on. As long as something is blooming and nectar is flowing, worker bees will fly many miles each day to retrieve the sugar-rich fluid they transform in the cells of the hive into honey. In autumn, Earl's bees worked goldenrod and aster. Earlier in the year, they had gone for clover, which makes a mild, pleasant honey. Dark honey from the flowers of the tulip poplar, a common tree in the park, is also an early honey.

Then, there's sourwood honey. From late June through July, bees are abuzz around the blossoms of the sourwoods. This tree's kinship with other heath plants such as dog hobble is apparent in the white, lily-of-the-valley-like blossoms. The higher-elevation sourwoods, those between 2,000 and 3,500 feet, are said to be the best nectar producers.

Clear, golden sourwood honey is considered nectar of the gods in the mountains. Near-perfect sourwood, declared Knoxville writer Carson Brewer, has "the color of champagne" and a "tingly, sweet-tart taste." Sourwood honey is in high demand and fetches a fair price because it's not always abundant. Sometimes honey is labeled sourwood, but buyers should beware. Earl Ramsey said he can tell by the honey's smell whether it's the real thing—it has the fragrance of the sap of a sourwood tree. Some older folks say the only honey better than sourwood was that produced from the now-vanished American chestnut.

Raw honey was packed, comb and all, into jars. Some was kept for household use, for baking, sweetening beverages and fruit, and, of course, for lacing a hot buttered biscuit or chunk of cornbread. In a good year, honey was a valuable item to sell as well.

All this talk about sweet things brings up the topic of cakes. There were plain cakes, pound cakes, chocolate cakes, and coconut cakes, but in the mountains *the* quintessential cake, the highest expression of the art, was apple stack cake.

A stack cake consists of a multilayer, tortelike dessert of thin layers of cake with spiced apple filling spread between each layer. Different people had particular ways of making a stack cake: some recipes specify home-dried apples sweetened with molasses. A real stack cake artist sculpted the dough, much akin to sugar cookie dough, into perfect circles by hand rather than conforming them to a pan. And the more layers the better—a masterpiece towering eight or twelve layers high was not uncommon. Florence Cope Bush wrote that a stack cake was the centerpiece of the table at her grandparents' wedding celebration in 1898. Each woman attending the wedding brought a layer to add to the cake; the height of the cake was a measure of the bride's prominence and popularity.

Often, a cook reserved a special bowl for mixing cakes, and some insisted the batter should always be stirred in only one direction. The same soft, fine flour that made such exquisite biscuits was also used in cakes.

The list of desserts goes on and on . . . a panoply of pies, puddings, cookies, and cobblers. Never need a sweet tooth go unsated in the Smoky Mountains.

## Old-fashioned Stack Cake

Martha Whaley,
Gatlinburg, TN,
*Gatlinburg Recipe
Collection*

2 c. sugar
1 c. butter or shortening
2 eggs
1 tsp baking soda

3 tsp baking powder
6 c. flour (plain)
1 tsp vanilla
$^1/_2$ c. buttermilk

Cream sugar and butter together. Add eggs one at a time, beating well after each addition. Measure flour, sift with other dry ingredients, add to batter, alternating with buttermilk and vanilla. Divide into six or eight parts. Use a well-floured board to roll out mixture, or pat into well-greased 9-inch pans. Bake at 400 degrees until nice and brown.

**APPLE FILLING**

1 lb. dried apples
1 c. brown sugar
1$^1/_2$ tsp cinnamon

$^1/_2$ tsp cloves
$^1/_2$ tsp allspice

Cook apples and mash thoroughly. Add sugar and spices. Cool before spreading between layers.

## Apple Stack Cake

Lois Caughron,
Cades Cove, TN,
from Lois' mother,
Laura Anthony
Shuler

1$^3/_4$ c. white sugar
1 c. butter or shortening
1$^1/_4$ c. molasses or brown
    sugar
2 eggs
1 tsp vanilla
$^1/_2$ c. buttermilk

1 tsp soda
3 tsp baking powder
$^1/_2$ tsp cinnamon
$^1/_2$ tsp nutmeg
Pinch of salt
6 c. all-purpose flour

Preheat oven to 375 degrees. Cream sugar and shortening. Add molasses, vanilla, and eggs, beat thoroughly. Sift together dry ingredients. Add alternately with milk. Divide batter into 6 equal parts and shape into 6 balls. Place into 8- or 9-inch greased, floured cake pans. Pat dough to edge or roll and cut to size. Cool and stack with cooked, dried apples sweetened to taste. Better after sits day or so.

## Stack Cake

Mrs. Ollie
Lawhern,
Maryville-Alcoa
Times

*³/4 c. sugar*
*¹/4 c. butter*
*1 egg, beaten*
*¹/4 c. molasses*
*1 c. flour*
*1 tsp baking powder*

*³/4 tsp baking soda*
*¹/4 tsp nutmeg*
*¹/4 tsp allspice*
*¹/2 tsp cinnamon*
*¹/4 tsp salt*
*¹/4 c. buttermilk*

Cream sugar and butter and egg. Beat well. Mix in molasses. Sift together flour, baking powder, soda, spices, and salt. Mix into the butter mixture, alternating with buttermilk. Add more flour if necessary to make stiff dough. Knead on floured board. Divide into five portions. Pat each part out in a greased, floured cake pan. Bake about 10 minutes at 370 degrees. Spread cooked, dried, sweetened fruit (usually apples), between each layer.

## Mama's Basic Cake Recipe

Beuna Winchester,
Bryson City, NC

*2 c. flour*
*1 c. sugar*
*2-finger pinch soda*
*3-finger pinch baking powder*

*1 tsp salt*
*¹/2 c. shortening, worked in with fingers*
*2 eggs, separated*
*Milk*

Mama sifted the dry ingredients in a big round sifter into a big dishpan used only for that purpose. Stir eggs yolks into dry ingredients. Add enough milk to make soft batter. Stir with big wooden spoon, in one direction only, scrape bowl in that direction too. "We would get to lick the bowl and the spoon," said Beuna. Bake in cake pans at 350 degrees.

(Use egg whites for Seven-Minute Icing: Boil sugar and water and pour over egg whites; beat until stiff.)

## Dried Apple Fruit Cake

Louise Woodruff,
Walland, TN

$2^1/2$ c. hot apples
2 sticks butter
4 c. flour
4 tsp soda
1 c. nuts

2 c. sugar
1 tsp cinnamon
1 tsp allspice
2 eggs

Add butter to hot apples. Mix all other ingredients except eggs and add to butter and apples. Beat eggs and add. Pour into tube pan and bake at 350 degrees for one hour.

---

## Louise's Piecrust

Louise Woodruff,
Walland, TN

*Flour, White Lily
Self-Rising*

$^1/2$ c. buttermilk
$^1/3$ c. shortening

Sift bowl full of flour, make well in center, add buttermilk and shortening. Dip in and mix together with hands to make a very stiff batter, then let set about 10 minutes. Work back down and roll out thin on floured board to fit pie pan. Pour pie mixture in. This dough can also be used for fried pies.

---

## Buttermilk Pie

Kate Wade,
Sevierville, TN,
*Gatlinburg Recipe
Collection*

1 Tbsp flour
1 c. sugar
2 tsp nutmeg
3 egg yolks, well beaten (save whites)

2 Tbsp butter, melted
$^1/2$ c. buttermilk (add 1/4 tsp
soda)

Mix flour, sugar, and nutmeg together; add beaten egg yolks, melted butter, and milk. Bake in unbaked crust at 325 degrees until set. Beat whites of eggs into meringue, using 2 tablespoons of sugar per egg white. Spread on top, and brown slightly in oven.

---

## Butterscotch Pie

2 c. brown sugar
1 Tbsp butter
4 Tbsp flour

2 c. milk
3 egg yolks

Brown one cup of the sugar in butter in heavy skillet, adding a little boiling water. Mix the other cup of sugar with flour and add milk. Put in top of double boiler. Add the caramelized sugar. Stir well, cook 20 minutes. Slightly beat egg yolks and add, little by little, the hot mixture to eggs. Return and cook for 2 minutes. Pour into baked pie shell. (I do not think we packed brown sugar in measuring cup.)

Mary Ruble,
*Reminiscing With Recipes*

---

*1/4 lb. butter*
*1/2 c. brown sugar*
*1 c. white sugar*
*3 eggs*

*1 Tbsp vinegar*
*1/2 Tbsp vanilla*
*1 Tbsp cornmeal*

## Chess Pie

Lucinda Ogle,
Gatlinburg, TN

Melt butter and sugars, add eggs and other ingredients and stir until mixed. Do not beat. Bake in unbaked pie shell for one hour at 350 degrees.

---

*2 eggs*
*1 1/2 c. brown sugar*
*2 Tbsp cornmeal*

*2 Tbsp water*
*Vanilla*
*Lump of butter size of walnut*

## Cornmeal Pie

John D. Webb,
Townsend, TN

Mix all ingredients together and pour into pie shell. Bake at 350 degrees for 25-30 minutes.

---

*1/2 c. flour*
*1/2 tsp allspice*
*1/2 tsp salt*
*1/2 tsp cinnamon*
*1/2 c. brown sugar*

*1 c. sour milk*
*1/2 tsp soda*
*3/4 c. molasses*
*2 eggs*
*2 Tbsp butter, melted*

## Molasses Pie

Faye Ownby,
Sevierville, TN,
*1971 Home Demonstration Club Cookbook*

Sift together dry ingredients, except baking soda. Put in sour milk. Mix molasses and add other dry ingredients, including

soda. Add eggs and butter. Beat until smooth. Pour into flaky
crust and bake at 375 degrees 45 minutes to one hour.

---

**Molasses
Pie**

(Mountain Trails)

1 c. sugar
2 c. molasses
3 eggs

1 Tbsp melted butter
Juice of one lemon
Pinch of nutmeg

Mix all ingredients together and heat. Pour into piecrust and
bake at 350 degrees for 45–50 minutes.

---

**Old-
fashioned
Pumpkin
Custard
Pie**

Lois Caughron,
Cades Cove, TN

2 eggs
1 can (1 lb.) pumpkin,
   fresh or canned
3/4 c. sugar
1/2 tsp salt
1/2 tsp cinnamon
1/2 tsp ginger

1/4 tsp allspice
1/4 tsp cloves
2 cans (6 oz. size) evaporated
   milk
3 Tbsp molasses
1 egg white

Preheat oven to 400 degrees. Beat eggs until frothy, add
remaining ingredients, except egg white. Place unbaked, 9-inch
pie shell on lowest rack of oven, pour in filling. Bake 55–60 minutes. Cool on wire rack. Garnish with whipped cream and nuts.

---

**Pumpkin
Pie**

Louise Woodruff,
Walland, TN

Louise and her husband, Charles, have a whole yard full of
pumpkins for sale in the fall at their home in Walland,
Tennessee, on the edge of the Smokies. The traditional bright
orange pumpkin everyone associates with Halloween is *not* the
best cooking pumpkin. The best pumpkin for cooking, according
to the Woodruffs, is the old-fashioned, dusty-orange field
pumpkin. They also grow cushaws, a green striped squash. Louise
is famous for her pumpkin and cushaw pies. Though the filling
contains no evaporated milk, the texture of this pie is silky

smooth and absolutely delicious. Here's how Louise makes it:

First, peel the pumpkin or cushaw, cut up into pieces, add water, cook until real tender. Drain water off.

For one pie:

| | |
|---|---|
| 3 c. pumpkin or cushaw | 1 stick margarine, melted |
| 1 c. white sugar | 1 Tbsp vanilla |
| 1 c. brown sugar | 3 Tbsp flour or cornstarch |
| 4 eggs | |

Mix all ingredients together and beat well with spoon or mixer, pour into two unbaked 9-inch pie shells. Bake 30 minutes at 400 degrees.

### Apple Pie

Louise Woodruff,
Walland, TN

| | |
|---|---|
| 6–7 c. apples, peeled | ³/4 to 1 c. sugar |
| (Winesaps or Romes) | ¹/2 to 1 tsp cinnamon |

Cook and mash apples, put in sugar and cook down, then add cinnamon. Put into two piecrusts and put crust on tops. With fork, pierce holes in tops. Bake at 425 degrees for 50 minutes.

### Vinegar Pie

Sidney Saylor Farr,
*More Than
Moonshine*

| | |
|---|---|
| 1 c. sugar | 2 Tbsp flour |
| 1 c. water | 1 Tbsp butter |
| 2 eggs | ¹/2 tsp lemon extract |
| 2 Tbsp vinegar | 1 9-inch baked piecrust |

Stir together sugar, water, eggs, vinegar, and flour in top of double boiler. Cook, stirring constantly until mixture is thick and smooth. Remove from heat and stir in butter and lemon extract. Turn into baked pie shell. Let cool. Top with whipped cream if desired.

## Egg Pie

Mrs. Ollie
Lawhern,
Maryville-Alcoa
Times

4 good-sized eggs
1 1/2 c. sugar or molasses
Pinch of salt
1 c. "top" milk

2 Tbsp cornmeal
1 tsp vanilla
Big pinch (1/4 tsp) fresh-shaved
    nutmeg

Break the four eggs into a bowl and beat well. Then beat in sugar, salt, milk, cornmeal, vanilla, and nutmeg. Pour into un-cooked piecrust and bake in an "easy oven" (350 degrees). Makes a 10-inch pie. Mrs. Lawhern says they cooked it as custard without piecrust, sweetened with honey and without cornmeal.

## Ol' Timey Fried Pies

Beuna Winchester,
Bryson City, NC

These pies are also good with a filling of mincemeat or any thick preserves, such as peach and others. Some fancy people sprinkle powdered sugar on top of their pies after they are cool.

Dried apples
Pastry dough

Fat

Stew dried apples (or any other dried fruit). Drain off all juice, mash well, and sweeten to taste. Roll out a rich pastry dough and cut into 5- or 6-inch circles. Place the cooked fruit in the center of the dough circles, leave a margin around edges. Fold over, moisten edges so they stick together with a fork. Fry in hot deep fat, about 350 to 375 degrees, or fry in small amount of fat in a frying pan. Turn pies so they will brown on both sides.

## Rhubarb Pie

Mrs. Glenn
Shelton,
Sam Houston
Schoolhouse
Cookbook

1 c. sugar
2 Tbsp flour (heaping)
1/2 c. cream or milk
1 tsp. vanilla

1 c. rhubarb, diced
2 egg yolks (save whites for
    meringue)
Butter, size of an egg

Mix all ingredients together and pour into an unbaked pie shell and bake slowly for 45 minutes. For meringue, beat whites with 4 tablespoons sugar until peaks form and put on top, brown in 350-degree oven.

Both of the following recipes using fresh-picked blackberries have been "tried and tested by Faye Cardwell . . . loved and delighted by Glenn Cardwell." Glenn notes that the "real first step in preparing either is to have husband go to the fields and pick a half gallon of berries."

**Blackberry Dumplings & Blackberry Pie**

Glenn Cardwell, Greenbrier, TN

## BLACKBERRY DUMPLINGS

| | |
|---|---|
| 1 quart berries | 3/4 c. sugar |
| 1 quart water | 1/2 stick butter or margarine |

Put blackberries and water on to cook in big pot. When they are cooked, add sugar and butter.

Dumpling Dough:

| | |
|---|---|
| 2 c. self-rising flour (if using plain flour, add 3 tsp baking powder and teaspoon of salt) | 6 Tbsp shortening |
| | 2/3 c. milk |

Mix flour and shortening with fork and add milk. Dip out dough one tablespoon at a time and drop into center of boiling berry mixture. After all the dough is dropped in, cover, reduce heat to low, and cook 8–10 minutes. Although Faye rolls out the dough, Glenn likes to make them as his mother did by just dropping them from spoon. Be sure the berries are boiling. DO NOT STIR, because it will "lump the dumplings together and you've got a mess." When the dumplings are done, dip off with a big spoon and put in dessert dish. Makes two day's worth for four people.

## BLACKBERRY PIE

Filling:

| | |
|---|---|
| 4 c. blackberries | 1/4 tsp nutmeg |
| 2 Tbsp plain flour | 1/8 tsp salt |
| 3/4 c. sugar | 1/2 tsp cinnamon |

Combine the berries, flour, sugar, and spices and let sit until sugar dissolves. You can make the crust during this time.

Crust:

> $2^1/4$ c. plain flour      $2/3$ c. shortening
> 1 tsp salt

Cut shortening into dry ingredients and add enough cold water until dough sticks together. Roll out two crusts. After placing bottom crust into pie pan, pour berry filling into crust and place top crust on. Bake at 350 degrees for one hour.

---

**Sweet Potato Pie**

Beuna Winchester,
Bryson City, NC

> 4 c. mashed cooked sweet    2 Tbsp flour
>    potato (can also use      1 tsp salt
>    pumpkin)      1 c. buttermilk
> 4 Tbsp butter or      $1/2$ tsp baking soda
>    margarine, softened      2 tsp vanilla
> 4 eggs      2 unbaked 9-inch pie shells
> 2 c. sugar

Combine sweet potato, butter, and eggs and mix well. Combine sugar, flour, and salt and stir into potato mixture. Combine buttermilk and baking soda, add to potato mixture, and mix well. Stir in vanilla. Pour filling into pastry shells. Bake at 350 degrees one hour and 10 minutes, or until set.

---

**Quickie Peach Cobbler**

Lucinda Ogle,
Gatlinburg, TN

> 1 c. flour      1 c. milk
> 2 tsp baking powder      3 or 4 c. cooked, sliced peaches,
> Pinch salt      drained
> 1 c. sugar

Sift flour, baking powder, and salt together. Mix in sugar and milk, pour in large glass baking dish, lay on peaches, bake at 350 degrees until brown, about one hour; dough will come up through peaches. "This is right tasty," said Ephraim Maples. "We just eat it all up."

1 stick margarine
2 c. sugar
2 c. water
1 1/2 c. self-rising flour
1/2 c. shortening

1/2 c. milk
2 cups chopped apples, about
   6 apples, use tart apples such
   as Granny Smiths or Winesaps
1 tsp cinnamon

**Mom's
Apple
Cobbler**

Beuna Winchester,
Bryson City, NC

Heat oven to 350 degrees. Melt margarine in 13x9x2 pan. In saucepan, heat sugar and water until sugar melts. Cut shortening into flour until resembles fine crumbs. Add milk and stir with fork until dough leaves sides of bowl. Roll dough into a large rectangle. Sprinkle cinnamon over apples. Spread apples evenly over dough. Roll up like jelly roll. Dampen edge of dough with water to seal. Slice into 16, 1/2-inch pieces and place in pan with melted margarine. Pour sugar syrup carefully around rolls. Bake 55–60 minutes.

1 c. sugar
1 Tbsp butter
2 c. hot water
2 c. sliced peaches

1 c. flour
2 tsp baking powder
1/2 tsp salt
2 c. milk or cream

**Peach
Dumplings**

Lucinda Ogle,
Gatlinburg, TN

Make syrup with sugar, butter, and hot water. Add peaches. Let this come to boil. Make dumplings by mixing flour, baking powder, and salt into stiff batter with milk. Drop large spoonfuls of batter into boiling syrup and peaches. Cover and cook for 20 minutes. Spoon out dumplings and fruit into bowl and serve with cream or milk if desired. Blackberries or other fruits can also be used.

**Aunt Lindy's Sweet Bread or Biscuits**

Lucinda Ogle, Gatlinburg, TN

On Christmas morning Aunt Lindy (Lucinda Ogle's great-aunt) gave these cookies to all the children who came to her house on Le Conte Creek. Lucinda and a half dozen others would knock on Aunt Lindy's door and yell "Christmas gift." Because they yelled it first, they got the gifts.

Aunt Lindy, Lucinda recalled, was a plump, jolly woman, and Uncle George said "it was a good thing everybody didn't see alike, or they'd all want his Lindy."

| | |
|---|---|
| $^1/_2$ c. butter | 1 tsp baking powder |
| 1 c. sugar | $^1/_2$ tsp baking soda |
| 2 eggs | $^1/_2$ tsp salt |
| 1 tsp vanilla | $^1/_2$ c. buttermilk |
| 3 c. flour (plain) | |

Cream butter and sugar together. Add eggs and vanilla. Sift together flour, baking powder, soda, and salt. Add buttermilk alternately with dry ingredients. The dough should be as soft as you can handle. Divide and roll on floured board about $^1/_3$ inch thick. Cut in shapes with biscuit cutter. Sprinkle with coarse sugar, grate fresh nutmeg over top. Bake at 400 degrees until lightly browned.

---

**Molasses Cookies**

(Mountain Trails)

| | |
|---|---|
| 1 c. shortening | 3 c. sifted flour |
| 1 c. sugar | 1 tsp each cinnamon, ginger, |
| 1 egg | and salt |
| $^1/_2$ c. molasses | $^1/_2$ tsp mace |
| $^3/_4$ tsp vinegar | 2 tsp baking soda |
| $^3/_4$ c. milk or cream | |

Cream shortening and sugar, add well-beaten egg. Add molasses and beat well. Combine vinegar and milk. Sift dry ingredients and add alternately with milk mixture. Drop by tablespoons about two inches apart on greased cookie sheets. Bake at 350 degrees 8–10 minutes. Makes about six dozen cookies.

2³/4 c. White Lily
 Self-rising Flour
1 tsp baking soda
1 tsp each cinnamon
 and ginger

¹/4 tsp cloves
1 c. packed brown sugar
³/4 c. margarine, softened
1 egg
¹/4 c. light molasses

**Old-fashioned Ginger Snaps**

Lois Caughron,
Cades Cove, TN

Combine flour, soda, spices, and set aside. Cream sugar and margarine. Beat in egg and molasses until light and fluffy. Stir in flour mixture until just blended. Chill thoroughly. Preheat oven to 375 degrees and lightly grease baking sheets. Shape dough into ³/4-inch balls, and roll in granulated sugar. Place on sheets 2 inches apart, flatten with bottom of glass dipped in sugar. Bake 8–10 minutes or until cookies are set. Cool. Makes about 8 dozen.

---

2 c. brown sugar
4 eggs, well beaten
¹/2 c. flour

¹/2 tsp salt
¹/2 tsp baking powder
2 c. chopped walnuts

**Black Walnut Cookies**

Ferne Shelton,
Southern
Appalachian
Mountain
Cookbook

Mix brown sugar and eggs. Add flour, salt, and baking powder. Stir in the chopped nuts. Drop by teaspoonfuls onto greased baking sheet. Bake at 375 degrees about 12 minutes.

---

1¹/2 c. sorghum molasses
¹/2 c. sugar
¹/2 c. water

Stick of butter
Pinch of baking soda

**Molasses Candy**

(Mountain Trails)

Put sugar and molasses in saucepan, add ¹/2 c. water. Stir until dissolved. Cook until small, hairlike strings of syrup fall from the spoon. Add the butter and baking soda, stir. Pour into buttered bowl. Grease hands well and pick up candy when cool enough. Pull and fold over like taffy until golden. Pour onto plates, let spread, then cut into squares to cool.

## Popcorn Balls

Louise Woodruff,
Walland, TN

| | |
|---|---|
| 1 c. sugar | 1 tsp salt |
| 1/4 c. sorghum | 1 Tbsp butter |
| 1/4 c. water | 2 quarts popcorn |

Combine first five ingredients in saucepan, cook to hard ball stage (250 degrees F.), stirring occasionally. Remove from heat. Quickly stir in popped corn and turn out into buttered pan. Shape quickly with buttered hands into balls and set on waxed paper to cool. Makes six popcorn balls.

---

## Brownies

Louise Woodruff,
Walland, TN

| | |
|---|---|
| 5 Tbsp melted butter or margarine | 1/2 c. White Lily flour |
| 1/3 c. cocoa | 1/4 tsp salt |
| 2 eggs slightly beaten | 1 tsp vanilla |
| 1 c. sugar | 3/4 c. nuts |

Blend melted margarine with cocoa to form a paste. Beat eggs and sugar until light yellow. Blend in cocoa and margarine mixture. Beat well. Add flour, salt, and vanilla. Blend until smooth. Pour into greased 8-inch pan. Sprinkle nuts over batter. Bake in 350-degree oven 30–35 minutes. Cool completely before cutting.

---

## Gingerbread

Sue Cox, extension
agent, Agricultural
Extension Service,
Knoxville, TN

| | |
|---|---|
| 1/2 c. sugar | 1/2 tsp salt |
| 1/2 c. shortening | 1 1/2 tsp baking soda |
| 1 beaten egg | 1 tsp ginger |
| 1 c. sorghum | 1 tsp cinnamon |
| 2 1/2 c. sifted flour | 1 c. hot water |

Cream sugar and shortening; add egg and sorghum; beat well. Add sifted dry ingredients; mix well. Add hot water and mix. Pour batter into greased 9x12 pan; bake at 350 degrees for 35 minutes.

Beat together:

| | |
|---|---|
| 4 c. sugar | 1 c. cooking oil |
| 4 c. pumpkin | |

Sift together and add to first mixture:

| | |
|---|---|
| 5 c. flour | 1 tsp cloves |
| 1 tsp cinnamon | 1 c. nuts |
| 1/2 tsp salt | 1 egg |
| 4 tsp soda | 1 c. raisins |

Bake one hour at 350 degrees in greased bread pans. Makes three loaves.

## Pumpkin Bread

Louise Woodruff,
Walland, TN

---

| | |
|---|---|
| Biscuit batter | Milk |
| Pint fresh blackberries | Sugar |

Make a thin biscuit batter, add blackberries into dough, and bake in big cooking pan. Pour sweet dip, a mix of milk and sugar, over top.

## Blackberry Pudding with Sweet Dip

Bonnie Myers,
Townsend, TN

---

"City slickers" call them blueberries—they may be obtained frozen in markets the year 'round. We pick them fresh in the mountains.

| | |
|---|---|
| 1 egg | 1 c. sugar |
| 1/2 c. milk | Pinch of salt |
| 1 tsp vanilla | 3 level tsp baking powder |
| 2 Tbsp shortening | 1 1/3 c. huckleberries |
| 2 1/2 c. flour | |

Beat egg. Add milk, vanilla, and shortening. Mix together flour, sugar, salt, and baking powder. Slowly add to first mixture. Wash berries, then drain and roll in flour and stir in gently to keep them whole. Bake in 8-inch skillet 55 minutes at 250 degrees until done.

## Huckleberry Pudding

Elsie Burrell,
Maryville, TN,
Sam Houston
Schoolhouse
Cookbook

## Creamy Rice Pudding

Lois Caughron,
Cades Cove, TN

1 1/2 c. cooked rice,
    leftover from breakfast
2 c. milk
1/3 c. sugar
1/4 tsp salt

1 egg, beaten
2/3 c. raisins
1 Tbsp margarine
1/2 tsp vanilla
Dash nutmeg and cinnamon

Combine rice, 1 1/2 cups of the milk, sugar, and salt in heavy saucepan. Cook over medium heat, stirring occasionally until thick and creamy, about 15 to 20 minutes. Blend remaining 1/2 cup milk, and the egg. Stir into rice mixture. Add raisins. Cook 2 minutes longer, stirring constantly. Add margarine and vanilla. Put into dishes. Eat warm or cool.

---

## Persimmon Pudding

Lucinda Ogle,
Gatlinburg, TN

1 pint persimmons
1 tsp baking soda stirred
    into pulp
3/4 c. sugar

1 c. flour
1/2 stick margarine or butter,
    melted
1 egg beaten

Harvest persimmons after first good frost in autumn. Peel, wash, and run one pint of persimmons through a sieve. Stir ingredients together and bake at 350 degrees until brown, about 30 minutes.

---

## Persimmon Pudding

Ferne Shelton,
*Southern*
*Appalachian*
*Mountain*
*Cookbook*

2 c. persimmon pulp
3 beaten eggs
1 1/2 c. sugar
1 1/2 c. flour
1 tsp baking powder
1 tsp baking soda

1/2 tsp salt
3/4 c. milk
1/2 tsp each cinnamon and
    allspice
1 tsp vanilla

Persimmons are ready after first frost. To prepare pulp, select and wash ripe persimmons. Mash well, adding small amount of water if necessary; put through colander. To the 2 cups of pulp, add remaining ingredients and mix well. Pour into buttered dish and bake at 350 degrees for 1 hour. To serve, cut in squares and top with whipped cream.

2 c. flour
2 tsp baking powder
1/2 tsp each salt and
      baking soda

2 Tbsp melted shortening
1/2 c. buttermilk
1/2 c. molasses
1 egg

**Molasses Muffins**

Ferne Shelton,
Southern
Appalachian
Mountain
Cookbook

Mix dry ingredients, add shortening, buttermilk, molasses and egg. Stir until just moistened. Pour into hot, greased muffin tins. Bake at 400 degrees for 25 minutes.

---

1 egg
1 Tbsp sugar
1 tsp salt
1 c. milk

1 tsp baking powder
2/3 c. flour
4 to 6 apples, cored
Lard or shortening for frying

**Apple Fritters**

Sidney Saylor Farr,
More Than
Moonshine

Beat egg well, add sugar and salt, then milk, alternately with flour (in which baking powder has been sifted). Mix well. Cut each apple into four slices across and dip in batter. Put lard or shortening at least an inch deep in heavy skillet. Fry apple slices until dough is golden brown.

---

Apples, raisins, currants,
      candied fruits
Molasses
Apple juice

Sugar
Spices
Beef or suet

**Mincemeat**

Stacy Tuggle,
Norris, TN

Mix together chopped apples, raisins, currants, candied fruits, molasses, apple juice, and sugar. Add spices (cloves, nutmeg, cinnamon, salt and pepper). Then chop up roast beef or use suet. Mix and cook slowly for a few hours. Seal in hot jars and use as filling for pies.

# PICKLES, RELISHES, PRESERVES, & BUTTERS

### OF THE SMOKIES

# Pickles, Relishes, Preserves, & Butters

"The real recipe for pickling is a cup of sugar, a cup of vinegar, and a cup of water."

—Lucinda Ogle

Like hot salsas and tangy chutneys of other cultures, pickles, relishes, and preserves provide spicy sidelights to Smoky Mountain meals. Pickles and relishes are kissing cousins: pickles are usually vegetables left whole or cut in chunks, while relishes are combinations of finely chopped vegetables (or fruits). Both are preserved in solutions of salt brine and vinegar.

Pickles, both sweet and dill, are a favorite way to preserve fresh cucumbers—with the emphasis on fresh. For best results, cucumbers should not be more than twenty-four hours out of the garden before pickling; waiting longer will result in hollow or shriveled pickles.

*A pregnant woman cannot make pickles successfully.*

The way to make cucumber pickles has remained fairly constant through the centuries: soak cucumbers in a brine of soft water with pure pickling salt, boil in a vinegar and sugar solution, then store in barrels or crocks. (With the patent of the glass Mason jar in 1858, pickles could be put up in smaller quantities.) In the "short brine" method, pickles are soaked only a few hours. The "long brine" method involves many days of soaking and rinsing before processing the pickles. A white powdered sulfate called alum is included in some recipes for crisping pickles, but a grape leaf put in the jar has the same effect.

In the opinion of food writer John Egerton, "The cucumber seems made to be a pickle; nothing else makes a better one." And though cucumbers are the most common raw material of pickles, mountain people don't let other vegetables go to waste either—okra, cauliflower, and green tomatoes, among others, are main ingredients in unusual and delicious pickles.

The "zip" in pickles (and relishes) is due to the addition of various herbs and spices—dill, garlic, celery seed, mustard seed, nutmeg, turmeric, cloves, and some tongue-tingling, tear-inducing hot peppers. Whole spices are sometimes tied in a small cloth bag and removed before processing so the pickles don't become cloudy.

Salt and vinegar are the preservative agents in pickles and relishes. Salt deters spoiling by forming lactic acid. Vinegar's high acidity discourages the growth of bacteria that can cause food to go bad. (White vinegar, which mountain people had to buy, produced a lighter pickle. Cider vinegar, which they made themselves, resulted in a darker pickle.) Though not a preservative in the quantities used in pickles, sugar helps retain the texture, flavor, and color of foods.

Big crocks or jugs of vinegar were kept in every mountain cabin. This basic, useful liquid was made from fermented apples or apple cider. Bonnie Myers remembered her grandmother talking about making vinegar. She put rotting apples in a keg with water, then set them aside until a gel-like substance called the "mother" rose to the top. This was the signal the vinegar was done. The "mother," also called "vinegar plant," is an old term for the membrane that forms on the surface of a liquid during fermentation—it consists mostly of yeast cells and bacteria. Another common way to make vinegar was simply to let apple cider sit for

Vegetables, herbs, and flowers florish in the garden at the Oconaluftee Mountain Farm Museum. *by Mary Ann Kressig*

about five weeks, until it passed through the hard cider stage to vinegar. Each fall, Glenn Cardwell's family set aside three to five gallons of apple cider for two to three months until it became vinegar, which was used the following summer to make pickles. Glenn related a mountain riddle repeated by every generation concerning the "mother" on vinegar.

Question: What is older than its mother?

Answer: Vinegar.

Relishes can be made with corn, squash, and apple as the primary ingredients. Corn relish, a popular one, is an autumn preparation. Bonnie Myers said they would gather the last peppers, corn, and onions from the garden; with the addition of both red and green peppers "it was real pretty." Tennessee resident and cookbook compiler Richard Parrott advises, "If you want a taste of what Heaven will be like, wait for a cold snowy December day, cook up a pot of pinto beans, a pone of cornbread, a skillet-full of fried potatoes, slice an onion and open a jar of corn relish."

**Mountain folk canned everything from jams and jellies to pickles and chow chow.**

*by Mary Ann Kressig*

Chowchow is another colorful confetti of chopped vegetables. The word chowchow may derive from the Chinese term *cha*, which means "mixed." Chowchow goes back a long way—it appeared in a South Carolina "receipt" book in 1770. Normally, chowchow calls for green tomatoes, cabbage, peppers, and onions, but assorted other vegetables can easily be added to this lively condiment.

Cooks take full advantage of the bounteous berries and fruits by making jams, jellies, preserves, and butters: put up in small glass jars, the blackberry jam, strawberry preserves, and crab apple jelly were like jewels.

"Mercy," declared Bonnie Myers, "we'd pick those blackberries, later berries past ripe, and Mama'd make jam and jelly." She didn't use pectin (a commercial product that aids jelling), but instead went by the "cup for cup" rule of thumb—a cup of fruit or juice to a cup of sugar. Jams and jellies are judged done when they slough off the spoon "glassy like." In Cades Cove, where Bonnie was born and raised, they also made gooseberry preserves. They would "take a sheet and put it out under a tall gooseberry bush and just shake it. Used to, the mountains would burn and that's what brought on the good berries." There aren't many gooseberries anymore, Bonnie said, because the forest has grown in over the years.

*Put pennies in apple butter to keep it from sticking.*

Thick apple butter, brown as walnuts, is another sweet preserve that required the better part of a day to make. Many people prefer tart Sour Johns or Winesaps for apple butter. Several bushels of apples are peeled and quartered, put into a big brass or copper kettle with heated water or apple cider, and cooked over an open fire outdoors on a bright fall day. The apples must be stirred constantly to prevent scorching and sticking. The tool for this job is a wooden stirring stick with a six-foot-long handle, often constructed of tuliptree because the wood doesn't contain acid. After the apples are soft and cooked

**Missie King Oakley making apple butter at Twin Creeks.** *circa 1933 by Cliff Oakley*

to a sauce, molasses, or a generous amount of sugar, is added. Quills, or sticks, of cinnamon could be put in just before the butter was completely done. Lois Caughron of Cades Cove said her grandmother may have used apple cider in her apple butter, then she added sugar and cooked it about half a day, until it was so thick it could be sliced like butter. (Apple butter was stored in big crocks.)

Like a ribbon on a dress or a detail on a piece of furniture, these edible accompaniments are not essential to life. But they undeniably make it more enjoyable and more interesting.

## Home Canning

Canning hasn't changed much through the years, but a few new techniques and procedures have been devised. To ensure safe, edible food, the most current canning methods must be observed.

Older open-kettle and oven methods are generally taboo. High-acid foods such as fruits, most tomatoes, and pickles and relishes should be processed in a boiling-water bath for a designated amount of time. Boiling temperatures will kill bacteria or yeasts that might spoil these foods.

Low-acid or non-acid foods such as meats, vegetables, and a few newer tomato varieties require higher temperatures achievable only in a pressure cooker. Green beans need special care because of the potential for botulism poisoning. As an extra safeguard, low-acid canned foods should be removed from the jar and boiled 10 to 15 minutes before eating.

Glass jars should be sterilized and free of chips or cracks. Jars may be reused, but dome lids cannot; new rubber rings are essential for a firm seal. Jams, jellies, and preserves can be sealed with paraffin. Store canned foods in a cool, dark place.

The best sources for current information on canning and preserving foods are county extension offices, U.S. Department of Agriculture publications, jar manufacturers, and the latest edition of a classic book entitled *Putting Food By* (Stephen Greene Press).

**Lime Pickles**

Ruby Maples,
Sevierville, TN,
*Homespun Recipes*

| 2 c. lime (pickling lime, not the fruit) | 8 lbs. cucumbers, sliced crosswise 2 gallons cold water |

Put cucumbers in lime and water mix. Let stand for 24 hours. Take out and wash three or four times until water is clear. Let stand in cold water for three or four hours. Take out of water.

Mix:

| 9 c. sugar | 4 Tbsp salt |
| 2 quarts white vinegar | 3 Tbsp mixed spices |

Pour mixture over cucumbers. Boil for 15 minutes. Put pickles in jars and seal.

**Dill Pickles**

John D. Webb,
Townsend, TN

20–25 cucumbers (4- to 5-inch size, John D. likes Ashley Long Green). Wash cucumbers and soak in cold water overnight. The next morning, pack into hot sterilized quart jars. Into each jar measure:

| $^1/_8$ tsp powdered alum | Two heads fresh dill with seeds |
| Clove of garlic | One small hot red pepper. |

Combine:

| 1 quart vinegar | 3 quarts water |
| 1 c. canning salt | |

Boil mixture and fill each jar to top. Place washed grape leaf in top of each jar (for firmness and color). Add a little more vinegar and seal, allow to stand at least six weeks.

Dig root of Jerusalem artichoke (a sunflower) in fall. Scrape, slice, or use whole (if small) and soak in cold branch water (ice water), enough for 6 pints, for 3 hours.

**Jerusalem Artichoke Pickle**

Lucinda Ogle,
Gatlinburg, TN

Bring to a boil:

*1 quart vinegar*
*1/2 pint water*
*1 1/2 c. sugar*
*3/4 tsp white mustard seed*

*1 clove best garlic*
*1/2 c. salt*
*1/4 tsp crushed hot pepper*
*(optional)*

Dry off artichoke hearts. Put in sterilized jars and pour the boiling liquid over them. Ready to eat in 3 weeks. Better if put in refrigerator awhile to make crisp.

---

*2 lbs. small, tender, fresh
okra*
*5 hot red or green peppers
or crushed dried pepper*
*5 cloves garlic*

*1 quart white or apple cider
vinegar*
*1/2 c. water*
*6 tsp salt*
*1 tsp mustard seed*

**Pickled Okra**

John D. Webb,
Townsend, TN

Wash okra and pack in five hot jars. Put one pepper pod and clove of garlic in each jar. Bring remaining ingredients to boil. Pour over okra and seal. Let stand eight weeks before eating.

---

*3 lbs. young okra
(wash but do not cut)*
*Fresh dillweed and stems*
*1 quart water*

*1 pint white vinegar*
*Garlic cloves*
*1/2 c. salt*
*Red pepper (optional)*

**Pickled Okra**

Lucinda Ogle,
Gatlinburg, TN

Place sprigs of dill in bottom of pint jars. Pack washed, crisp, whole okra in jars. Do not cut off stems. Add boiling vinegar, garlic, salt to each pint.

## Green Tomato Pickles

John D. Webb,
Townsend, TN

| | |
|---|---|
| 2 gallons green tomatoes | 2 gallons vinegar |
| 1/2 gallon onions | 1 Tbsp black pepper |
| 6 c. sugar | 1 Tbsp salt |
| 1 c. hot peppers | |

Slice tomatoes and onions very thin. Put all ingredients in pot and boil about 20 minutes. Put in hot pint jars and seal. Makes about 12 pints.

---

## Virginia Chunk Pickles

Beuna Winchester,
Bryson City, NC

Making these pickles takes about two weeks and requires the following ingredients:

| | |
|---|---|
| Cucumbers | Sugar |
| Salt | Vinegar |
| Water | Pickling spices |
| Powdered alum | Celery seed |

Wash cucumbers and pack in jars. Make brine of 2 cups of salt to one gallon of water. Bring to boil and pour over cucumbers. Cover and let stand for one week. On the seventh morning, drain and cut into chunks. Put back into jars. Make a boiling solution of one gallon of water and one tablespoon powdered alum. Pour over chunks. Do this for three mornings. On the fourth morning, drain and make a solution of:

| | |
|---|---|
| 6 c. vinegar | 1/3 c. pickling spices |
| 5 c. sugar | 1 Tbsp celery seed |

Bring this solution to a boil and pour over pickles. On the fifth morning, drain this off in a pan. Add 2 cups sugar and heat to a boil. Pour over pickles. On the sixth morning, drain off again and add 1 cup sugar. Bring this to a boil. Pack pickles in jars. Pour liquid over the pickles. Seal.

Slice cucumbers and pour boiling water over them, enough to cover, and let stand for four hours. Make a solution of the following:

**Candied Dill Pickles**

Beuna Winchester, Bryson City, NC

$3^3/4$ c. vinegar        $4^1/2$ tsp mustard seed
6 c. sugar              $3^1/2$ Tbsp salt
$4^1/2$ tsp celery seed

Place head of dill in bottom of each jar, pack cucumbers in jars, and cover with boiling solution. Process in hot water bath for 5 minutes. Put a head of dill on top too.

---

1 gal. cucumbers        1 head cauliflower
10 small onions         Salt
5 stalks celery         Water
1 large sweet pepper     Alum, 2 boxes

**Cucumber & Cauliflower Pickles**

Louise Woodruff, Walland, TN

Slice about a gallon of cucumbers, add other vegetables, and put 1 pint salt to 1 gallon water. Leave 3 days in salt water. Drain cucumber mix. Place in plain water and soak overnight. Wash in clear water. Place 2 boxes alum in just enough warm water to dissolve and put over pickles. Add the rest of cold water to cover mix. Soak overnight. Rinse and place pickles in bottom of large crock.

For the pickling solution:
16 c. sugar             2 Tbsp mustard seed
10 c. vinegar           2 tsp celery seed
1 box pickling spice     2 tsp turmeric

Tie spices in white cloth. Bring vinegar and sugar to boil. Place spices in liquid and boil. Pour over pickles and let set overnight. Drain and bring liquid to boil. Pour liquid over pickles. Let mixture cool before covering. After third day, drain mixture and heat liquid to boiling. Put in jars, cover with hot liquid, and seal. Note: It takes 2 gallons of salt water to fill 5-gallon crock.

**Sweet Pickles**

Louise Woodruff, Walland, TN (this is her mother, Mae's, recipe)

*Two gallons cucumbers*
*About 1 1/4 oz. alum*

*About 1 1/4 oz. ginger*

Soak cucumbers in salt water for two weeks. Take out and wash and soak in clear water 48 hours. Cut in pieces 1/4 inch thick. Boil one half hour in 1/2 box alum. Drain and refill pot with cold water, then boil a half hour in 1/2 box of ginger.

Make syrup of:
*3 1/2 lbs. sugar*
*1 quart vinegar*

*1 quart water*
*Mixed pickling spices*

Boil pickles in syrup 10 minutes and can in jars.

---

**Universal Pickles**

Beuna Winchester, Bryson City, NC

This is a pickle relish.

*1 gallon vinegar*
*5 lbs. brown sugar*
*1 box ground mustard*
*1/2 c. salt*
*1/2 c. whole black pepper*

*1 dozen sticks of ginger*
*1/2 c. cloves*
*2 dozen green peppers, chopped*
*2 dozen small onions, chopped*
*Few pieces of horseradish*

Put all together in jars. Let stand for one week, stirring each day.

Then add:
*Chopped cucumbers*
*Chopped cabbage*

*Chopped green tomatoes*
*(or other vegetables may want)*

Seal in individual jars.

---

**Apple Relish**

Mrs. John H. Huff, Sevierville, TN, *Homespun Recipes*

*1 1/2 gallons apples, peeled and quartered*
*12–15 onions, peeled and chopped*
*12 red sweet peppers or more for color, chopped*

*6 green sweet peppers, chopped finely*
*2 c. vinegar*
*Hot peppers to taste*

Cook all ingredients until tender. (Do not add water). Can in hot jars and seal.

---

| | | **Corn** |
|---|---|---|
| 4 c. fresh corn | 4 c. vinegar | **Relish** |
| 5 c. chopped green peppers | 2 c. sugar | |
| 2 c. chopped onions | 1/4 c. salt | John D. Webb, |
| 2 c. sliced unpeeled | 1 Tbsp turmeric | Townsend, TN |
| cucumbers | 1 Tbsp mustard seed | |
| 4 c. chopped ripe tomatoes | | |

Combine vegetables. Add vinegar, sugar, salt, turmeric, and mustard seed. Heat to boiling, simmer 25 minutes or until the vegetables are tender. Seal in hot, sterilized jars. Makes six pints.

---

This is another version of corn relish without tomatoes or cucumbers or cabbage.

**Corn Relish**

Beuna Winchester,
Bryson City, NC

9 c. corn, boil and cut off cob

2 c. carrots, chopped and cooked

1 c. chopped onions

1 c. celery, chopped

2 c. red and green sweet peppers, chopped

Drain then add:

3 c. vinegar

1 tsp celery seed

1 1/2 c. water

1 Tbsp salt

2 1/2 c. sugar

Put all ingredients together and cook 10 minutes.

Then add:

1 tsp pepper

1 tsp turmeric

1 tsp dry mustard

Cook mixture 10 more minutes, pack in jars, and boil 5 minutes in water bath.

## Corn Relish

Louise Woodruff,
Walland, TN

Another variation on corn relish using cabbage and prepared mustard.

*Kernels from 12 ears corn*  *3 pods hot pepper*
*1 quart cider vinegar*  *1 medium cabbage*
*12 sweet peppers (6 red,*  *3 c. sugar*
*6 green)*  *1 Tbsp salt*
*12 onions*  *1 pint prepared mustard*

Cook corn and vinegar together 20 minutes. Then add all chopped ingredients, sugar, salt, and mustard. Cook for 15–20 minutes. Can and seal.

---

## Squash Relish

Louise Woodruff,
Walland, TN

Grind up:
*10 c. squash*  *2 large bell peppers*
*4 large onions*

Soak for 24 hours in ¹/₄ c. coarse salt. Wash and drain.

Add:
*1 jar pimentos*  *1 tsp turmeric*
*2¹/₂ c. vinegar*  *1 tsp nutmeg*
*4¹/₂ c. sugar*  *1 tsp black pepper*
*1 Tbsp cornstarch*  *1 Tbsp celery seed*

Cook for 30 minutes on low heat and put in hot jars and seal.

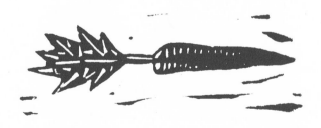

| 2 heads cabbage | 12 green peppers | **Chowchow** |
| 12 onions | $^1/_2$ c. salt | |
| 12 tomatoes | 4 c. water | Louise Woodruff, Walland, TN |

Chop and soak the above ingredients for 2 hours and drain.

Then add:

| 3 tsp mustard | 4 c. sugar |
| 3 tsp celery seed | 4 c. water |
| 4 c. vinegar | |

Cook all on medium heat until done, about 30 minutes, and put in hot sterilized jars.

This is the way Louise's mother made blackberry jelly.

**Blackberry Jelly**

Louise Woodruff, Walland, TN

| Blackberries | Sugar |

Wash berries, put in kettle with very little water. When boiled, put berries in cloth bag and let juice drain. Dispose of berries in cloth. Add sugar, cup for cup with juice. Boil and stir with wooden spoon. Use metal spoon to test for doneness: if jelly mixture slides off or drips with string between drips, then it's ready to put in jars. Seal each jar with paraffin.

---

| 1 quart fresh strawberries | 3 c. sugar |

**Strawberry Preserves**

Louise Woodruff, Walland, TN

Bring berries and 1 cup sugar to boil for 5 minutes, then add 2 cups sugar and boil 12 minutes. Put in crock or large bowl and let mixture cool, stirring occasionally to distribute berries. After cold, put in jars.

## Crab Apple Preserves

Crab apples
Water

$3^1/2$ c. sugar

Ferne Shelton, Southern Appalachian Mountain Cookbook

Peel and slice crab apples. Barely cover with water in covered pan and boil until fruit is soft. Drain through coarse sieve, then through a jelly bag. Mix 3 cups pulp and 1 cup juice in pan. Add sugar and cook until thick and smooth, about 20 minutes. Stir frequently to prevent sticking. Seal in jars while hot.

## Gooseberry Preserves

1 quart gooseberries
$^1/2$ c. water

4 c. sugar

Ferne Shelton, Southern Appalachian Mountain Cookbook

Wash gooseberries, add water. When boiling, add all the sugar. Boil quickly until berries are clear and juice is thick, about 15 minutes. Seal in jars.

## Peach Preserves

$^3/4$ lb. sugar
$^3/4$ c. water

1 lb. ripe peaches

Louise Woodruff, Walland, TN

Wash peaches, peel, and remove stones. Cut peaches in quarters. Boil sugar and water 10 minutes. Skim foam from top. Add fruit and cook quickly until peaches become transparent and clear. Seal in hot jars.

Tip for quick peach peeling: With slotted spoon, dip each peach into a pan of boiling water for a few seconds. The skin will slide right off.

## Peach Butter

Peaches

Sugar

Wash, peel, and remove pits from peaches. Crush peaches and cook in pot slowly until soft enough to mash. Add one cup of sugar to each cup of pulp and continue cooking, stirring constantly until sugar dissolves. Cook until mixture drops from spoon, then put in sterilized jars and seal with paraffin.

### Pickled Peaches

Cecily Brownstone, Associated Press Food Editor

3 lbs. ripe peaches
1 Tbsp mixed pickling spice, tied in cheesecloth bag
1 pint cider vinegar
1 lb. light brown sugar
2 lemons, unpeeled and thinly sliced
$^1/_2$ tsp salt

Cover peaches with boiling water and let stand about a minute; slip off skins. In large heavy saucepot, bring to a boil the spice, vinegar, sugar, lemon, and salt; simmer, uncovered, for 15 minutes. Add peaches and simmer until tender—about 10 minutes. Remove spice bag. Pack hot peaches into hot, sterilized jars. Fill with hot syrup leaving $^1/_4$-inch headspace. Add lids and seal according to jar manufacturer's directions. Process in boiling water bath for 15 minutes. Makes about 2 quarts.

## Pickled Crab Apples

Ferne Shelton, *Southern Appalachian Mountain Cookbook*

*6 c. vinegar*
*8 c. brown sugar*
*2 tsp cloves*

*1 stick cinnamon*
*8 lbs. crab apples*

Boil vinegar, brown sugar, cloves, and cinnamon together. Leave stems on crab apples. Add to syrup and boil until fruit is tender. Remove the fruit and pack into jars. Pour in syrup. Seal.

---

## Apple Butter

Duane Oliver, *Cooking on Hazel Creek*

This is a nineteenth-century recipe for an all-time mountain favorite.

*4 lbs. apples*
*2 c. water or cider*
*$^1/_2$ c. sugar*
*3 tsp cinnamon*

*1 $^1/_2$ tsp cloves*
*$^1/_2$ tsp allspice*
*Sugar to taste*

Stem and quarter the apples. Cook in the water or cider until soft. Strain and mash into a pulp. To each cup of pulp, add the sugar, stir in cinnamon, cloves, allspice, and additional sugar to taste. Cook over low heat, stirring often, until mixture slides off in sheets from spoon. Put up in jars.

---

## Apple Butter

Louise Woodruff, Walland, TN

*3 gallons apples*
*(Winesaps or Romes)*

*Sugar*
*$^1/_2$ tsp cinnamon oil*

Peel and quarter apples. Cook them and drain water. Add sugar to desired sweetness, cook until thick, and add cinnamon oil "when about ready to take it up." Makes enough for about a dozen pints. Louise does not, but some people do use cider or sorghum in making apple butter.

*3 c. applesauce*
*¹/₂ c. sugar*

*¹/₄ tsp nutmeg*

**Apple
Leather**

Mix applesauce, sugar, and nutmeg. Spread ¹/₂ inch thick in shallow pan. Bake in 250-degree oven about 3 hours. Take out when nearly dry and roll in powdered sugar if have it, like a jelly roll. Add nuts if desired. Slice thin and serve as a confection.

Ferne Shelton,
*Southern
Appalachian
Mountain
Cookbook*

BEVERAGES

OF THE SMOKIES

# BEVERAGES

"Here's to old corn likker—whitens the teeth, perfumes the
breath, and makes child birth a pleasure"
—North Carolina folk saying

Everybody knows people in the mountains made
moonshine. It was a fine, long-standing tradition. And whether
imbibed for its alcoholic value, or purely medicinal purposes,
a jug of moonshine was kept on hand in many households.

But moonshine wasn't an everyday beverage. What Smoky
mountain folk usually drank was nothing stronger than coffee,
tea, and milk. Once a year they'd make some apple cider or
eggnog.

But the true elixir of life was the simplest liquid of all—
pure spring water. It is difficult to overestimate the importance
of good water to mountain people. Every log cabin was located
near a "bold" spring that poured forth the best refreshment Earth
had to offer, free for the taking. The spring was walled in with
stone, and a structure called a springhouse was constructed over
the spring or just downstream to keep animals and debris out of
this precious source of water. Before electricity ran into the
mountains and refrigerators became commonplace, the
springhouse also served as the place where butter, milk, and eggs
were kept cool.

And though the cabins and springhouses are gone, former
Smokies residents still return to collect jugs of that clear
mountain spring water. To many, it is the source of a long and
healthy life.

With that good water they brewed strong black coffee and
many kinds of teas from woodland plants, including mint leaves,
sassafras root, and birch bark. Hubert Sullivan told of making
"spruce-pine" tea from the tips of the Eastern hemlock trees.

To make coffee, raw beans were purchased, parched at home
in a skillet, and ground in a hand-turned grinder as needed.
Bonnie Myers recalled hearing her mother, Viola Burchfield, say
her job when she was a child was to grind the coffee beans.

During the Civil War, coffee was unavailable when blockades cut off the supply. Resourceful mountain women found several unusual coffee substitutes. A pale brown beverage was brewed from toasted bread crumbs, and another cloudy drink was made from roasted sweet potatoes. They also gathered acorns and wild chicory roots, roasted them, and made coffeelike

Roy Davenport of Greenbrier Cove fetches water from a spring. *circa 1926 by Laura Thornborough*

beverages. Because of their high tannin content, acorns had to be leached in several waters, then browned and ground before suitable for consumption.

Nearly every mountain family had a milk cow, a most valuable animal. *The Compleat American Housewife 1776* contained helpful advice on "cow keeping by young housekeepers." It said "The first requisite is to have a good cow. One that has high hips, short forelegs, and a large udder is to be preferred." From that cow came the family's milk and butter. Lucinda Ogle described how they made butter and buttermilk. When they had enough cream to make a "churnin'" it was put in a warm place until it clabbered (tasted like sour cream). Then it was ready to churn. With a dasher churn "it took forever" to make firm butter. To get "puffy butter," which Lucinda preferred, she would take it out and add warm water. Puffy butter stretched farther for a big family. "We just put it out in a big dish and dipped it out with a big spoon," Lucinda said.

After the butter was taken out, the liquid left in the churn was buttermilk, in Lucinda's mind "the best buttermilk in the whole world." Icy cold from the springhouse, buttermilk was drunk as a beverage with meals, added to leftover cornbread and eaten like a cereal, and used in biscuits and other baked goods.

Apple cider was a treat in the fall. Apple grower John Dunn remembered going to his father's orchard in Dry Valley. They gathered apples off the ground and put them in a partitioned wagon and took them home to make apple cider. To do this, they ground up whole apples in a cider mill; the ground apples, called "pummies," were put into the tub and pressed into fresh, sweet cider with just the slightest tang. "I seen my daddy make a 60-gallon barrel of cider that would last until Christmas," Dunn said. "It was good cider."

Dorie Cope told how apple cider was made in the Smokies before 1912. The men spent months looking for a white, poplar log to serve as a cider press. When they found one just the right size, they hauled it in with a horse, stripped away the bark and limbs, hewed out one side, and bored a hole in the bottom. The hole was the spout from which the juice dripped. Apples were gathered and quartered and put into the "trough" in the log, then pounded with a round hickory mallet. When the apples were the consistency of course sand, a weight was put on them to force the juice down the spout and into a bucket. This juice was strained through a cloth. "Fresh cider didn't last long,"

Dorie recalled. It would ferment quickly and become hard cider which "can make you as drunk as moonshine."

A half cup of cider and half cup of honey made a drink called "switchell." It was kept in jar, and four teaspoons were added to a dipper of water for a thirst-quenching drink during the hot haymaking season.

Fruit brandies and wines were homebrewed in the mountains too. Apples, peaches, grapes, berries, and even the seed of the locust tree were all fermented into alcoholic beverages. Duane Oliver's great-great-grandfather, Moses Proctor, was the first settler in Possum Hollow on Hazel Creek. Right away, Moses planted a peach orchard on the hill above his cabin. As soon as the trees bore fruit, Moses made peach brandy.

In those days, the 1830s, it was legal to make and sell liquor. Census takers came around, and besides counting people and the amount of land a man owned, they also tallied how much brandy, wine, or liquor had been produced during the year. Moses "undoubtedly drank the peach brandy," Duane believed, "and most people added it or some form of alcohol to their homemade medicines. . . . It could, of course, be shared with census takers or anyone who stopped by."

One of the most famous moonshiners in the mountains was a man named Quill Rose. He was a neighbor of Duane Oliver's grandmother, Sadie Welch Farley, a teetotaling woman. But whenever Quill Rose stopped in for a visit, he would offer Sadie some of his "scorpion juice" for what ailed her.

Scorpion juice, panther sweat, white lightning, corn squeezins', moonshine—this powerful alcoholic drink brewed from corn has had many names attached to it, along with equal parts of myth and truth. In the early centuries in Ireland nearly everyone had a little still up in some wild glen. The Scotch-Irish naturally brought this tradition with them across the ocean to the Smoky Mountains. Corn in liquid form, they found, was much more profitable and easier to transport than dry corn.

In the late eighteenth century the federal government started levying taxes on whiskey, and in 1862 it became a federal offense to make whiskey without a license. Revenue agents swarmed over the mountains to locate illegal whiskey makers, and they met strong resistance every step of the way.

The words moonshine, and moonshiner, may have arisen because the product was manufactured at night by moonlight, or from "moonlighter," in Europe a person who smuggled brandy under cover of night. In the Smokies, moonshine earned a unique name—blockade—and a person who made it was a blockader. This usage, said author Michael Frome, may have derived from the Irish who had to run the English blockade.

The Great Smoky Mountains encompass over 800 square miles of rolling ridges and rushing streams. *by Mary Ann Kressig*

The Smoky Mountains provided everything a moonshiner needed—he would find a little out-of-the-way branch where red horsemint grew on the banks, a sign the water in the stream was soft. He'd conceal his still-house in a thick growth of laurel, so revenuers would have a hard time finding it. And of course he had no problem getting corn.

In 1918, the Eighteenth Amendment to the U.S. Constitution was adopted, and the era of Prohibition was underway. The Volsted Act was passed a year later to enforce the amendment, which was finally repealed in 1933. Both before and during Prohibition, though, Cades Cove was noted for whiskey production. A family feud developed there in the 1920s—stills were burned, people shot at each other, and one man finally was killed.

An estimated 95 percent of the residents of the Cataloochee area made their own liquor at one time, and Cosby, Tennessee, gained fame as the Moonshine Capital of the state. Audley Whaley, who hired on as a warden in 1940, was assigned to cover the entire eastern section of the new national park. He lived at Cosby and reported a still in every "holler" and whiskey stacked up everywhere. Whaley didn't bother any of those outside the park boundaries, but if he found one within the park, he'd leave a note and give them a deadline to remove their still. Although the distillers claimed the sale of corn whiskey kept their children from starving, Whaley enforced the law nevertheless. Most of the stills were moved.

*Whiskey by the gallon, Sugar by the pound, Great big bowl to put in, Spoon to stir it round.*

Moonshine was relatively easy to make, though the quality of the finished product varied widely depending on how much of a hurry a moonshiner was in. Choice white corn was the grain used in the mountains. Once sprouted, the corn was ground and mixed with cornmeal and honey, sugar, or molasses to make a sweet mash. Fermentation started, and once the mash turned sour, it was ready for cooking in the still. The liquid formed at this stage was called "corn beer." Some people couldn't resist a sip or two. But real moonshine required heating this liquid to 173 degrees Fahrenheit, the temperature at which alcohol vaporizes: the spirits of the fermented liquid separated from the water and rose up through the still's "arm" and into a long copper tube called the "worm." Surrounded by cold water, the vapor in the worm condensed and came out moonshine.

The first run, called "singlings," was weak and had to be put back in and redistilled in what was called the "doubling run." In an interview with author Joseph Dabney, a man named Arthur Young, born in 1903 under Clingmans Dome in the Smokies, said the doubling run was "when the alkihol comes. It'd be real *alkihol*." High proof. As the distilling continued, the proof dropped to a "good bead—about 100 proof."

To check the proof, the moonshine was put in a jar, shaken, and the "bead," or bubbles, were checked. If the liquor was properly potent, the bubbles should be about the size of BB shot. Some moonshiners would throw a tablespoon of this second run into the fire. If it didn't burn, it didn't have enough alcohol and should be run through a third time. If the liquor was ready, it was passed through a charcoal filter and you had yourself some pure moonshine, ready to drink if a person was in a real hurry. Around Gatlinburg, some people aged their whiskey by putting it into pickle barrels charred on the inside, tying a chain around the barrel, and letting it bob in a creek for about three weeks. This produced "a fine, red, well-aged whiskey," according to Dabney. Cheap, unaged whiskey with toxic additives was called rotgut or popskull.

Making moonshine was plain hard work, and it was little wonder, as Horace Kephart phrased it, that a blockader would sigh and say, "'Blockadin' is the hardest work a man ever done. And hit's wearin' on a feller's narves. Fust chance I git, I'm a-goin' ter quit!'"

Clear, cold water from a mountain spring was the most cherished drink of all. *by Mary Ann Kressig*

## Boiled Coffee

*2 level tablespoons coffee*   White of an egg
*to 3 cups water*

Duane Oliver,
*Cooking on Hazel Creek*

Grind the coffee moderately fine, add half the egg white to it and put into a perfectly clean coffee pot. Add enough cold water to moisten the coffee, then pour the measured water over, cover the pot closely and boil 10 minutes. Then pour in half a cup of cold water, draw the pot to the side of the range and allow it to stand 5 minutes to settle grounds before serving. Never let the coffee boil after the cold water has been added.

## Spruce-pine Tea

Hubert Sullivan,
Dry Valley, TN

Cut green tips of branches of the Eastern hemlock tree, steep in water as for tea, and sweeten to taste. Note, this hemlock is *not* the same plant that poisoned Socrates.

## Sassafras Tea

Thelma Phillips,
Norris, TN

People dug roots of sassafras trees in spring, often when clearing new ground. Wash the roots, split into pieces, leave bark on. Cover with water and boil until reaches "tea stage." Sweeten to taste. Can remove and reuse pieces of root to make tea later.

Gather small twigs when the first buds appear on the spicewood, boil in water. Serve hot. Sweeten if desired; molasses makes the best sweetening. Teas were also brewed from mints of all kinds, as well as birch bark and wintergreen.

**Spicewood Tea**

Aggie Ross Lossiah, Cherokee, NC, *Cherokee Cooklore*

---

In the 1800s, if a lemon were to be seen in the Smokies, it was only around Christmastime. Sumac lemonade was an ingenious substitute that provided a tangy, lemon-tasting drink, refreshing on a hot summer day.

Crush and immerse the red berries or "horns" of staghorn sumac in water. Let sit for a while, then strain, sweeten, and drink.

**Sumac Lemonade**

Sharon Elaine Hurst, *Our Smokies Heritage*

---

6 eggs, separated
3/4 c. sugar
1 pint heavy cream

1 pint sweet (whole) milk
1 pint brandy or whiskey
Nutmeg

**Eggnog**

Ferne Shelton, *Southern Appalachian Mountain Cookbook*

Beat eggs separately. Add 1/2 cup sugar to yolks and 1/4 cup sugar to whites. Mix and add heavy cream and sweet milk. Add brandy or whiskey slowly. Sprinkle nutmeg over top.

---

Bushel of apples

**Apple Cider**

Can vary kinds of apples depending on whether want a sweeter or more tart cider. Core and quarter apples, don't peel. Feed apples into hopper of cider mill, and catch pulp in container. Put the pulp into tub part of mill, wind down screw and press juice into another container. Strain through cloth. Drink fresh or chilled. Cider turns quickly into hard cider and then vinegar.

## Old Field Apricot Drink
### Oo-Wa-Ga

Aggie Ross
Lossiah,
Cherokee, NC
*Cherokee Cooklore*

Gather old field apricots (fruits of passion flower). Hull out the seeds and pulp, put on to boil after adding a tiny bit of baking soda to make the seeds separate from the pulp. Strain juice from the seeds and pulp, add cornmeal to juice and cook until meal is done.

---

## Hominy Corn Drink

Mrs. Clifford
Hornbuckle,
Cherokee, NC,
*Cherokee Cooklore*

Shell corn, soak in lye until the skins can be removed. Beat corn in the corn beater until it is size of hominy. Sift the meal from the corn particles. Cook the corn particles until done, adding a little cornmeal to thicken. Drink hot or wait until it sours and drink it cold. This drink may be kept for quite a while unless the weather is very hot. This was a customary drink to serve to friends who dropped by for a visit.

---

## Grape Juice

Ferne Shelton,
*Southern Appalachian Mountain Cookbook*

Pick over and wash grapes. Place in a kettle and barely cover with water. Boil until seeds are free. Strain and measure juice, then boil. Add 1/2 cup sugar to each quart of juice and boil 5 minutes. Bottle and seal tight.

---

## Red Grape Wine

Ferne Shelton,
*Southern Appalachian Mountain Cookbook*

Place grapes and clean stems in large pottery jar, mash and cover with a cloth. After 10 days or more fermentation, drain and press through cloth. Measure juice into pot, and add 2 1/2 pounds of sugar for every gallon of juice. Let stand until all bubbling stops, then seal in jars.

---

## Blackberry Wine

| | |
|---|---|
| *7 quarts blackberries, washed* | *7 lbs. sugar* |
| *3 1/2 quarts water* | *2 quarts water* |
| | *1 egg white* |

Add 3¹/₂ quarts water to mashed berries and let stand 24 hours. Strain. Beat egg white, add sugar and 2 quarts water. Boil 5 minutes and skim; cool. Add syrup to juice, stir, and put in cloth-covered jar. Skim for 10 mornings, then cover with cloth and let stand until fermentation stops. Bottle.

*Ferne Shelton, Southern Appalachian Mountain Cookbook*

---

## Elderberry Wine

*5 quarts fresh elderberries*     *6 quarts water*

Crush berries and place in a crock. Pour all water in with them. Stir once and cover. Let mixture stand two weeks, stirring once a day. At end of two weeks, measure the berry juice and add an equal amount of sugar. Return to crock and let stand two more weeks. Strain mixture through cheesecloth and pour into bottles. Cork, then bring out on a cold winter night.

*Sharon Elaine Hurst, Our Smokies Heritage*

## Moonshine

An old family recipe.

*1 peck shelled corn*          *25 lbs. sugar*
*25 lbs. cornmeal*             *¹/₃ lb. yeast*

*Sidney Saylor Farr, More Than Moonshine*

Put shelled corn in flour sack. Pour warm water over it, store in warm, dark place and keep wet several times each day. Watch for a few days, until corn starts to sprout. Let sprouts go until about two inches long. Spread out on flat spot to dry. When dry, grind sprouts and add the cornmeal, sugar, and boiled water to make a mash. Cool the mixture, then add yeast to a gallon of lukewarm water and pour into the mash. Add enough water to make 30 gallons of mash. Yeast speeds fermentation, and mash will be sour in about four days. Distill.

## SCIENTIFIC NAMES OF WILD PLANTS MENTIONED IN TEXT

acorn (*Quercus* spp.)

beargrass (*Yucca filiamentosa*)

birch bark (*Betula lenta*)

blackberry and raspberry (*Rubus* spp.)

brook or branch lettuce (*Saxifraga micranthidifolia*)

American chestnut (*Castanea dentata*)

cresses (dryland) (*Barbarea verna*)

cut-leaved toothwort (crow's foot) (*Cardamine concatenata*)

dock (*Rumex crispa*)

Eastern hemlock (*Tsuga canadensis*)

elderberry (*Sambucus canadensis*)

gooseberry (*Ribes* spp.)

green-headed coneflower (*Rudbeckia laciniata*)

huckleberry (*Gaylussacia* spp.)

Jerusalem artichoke (*Helianthus tuberosus*)

passion flower fruit (old field apricot) (*Passiflora incarnata*)

persimmon (*Diospyros virginiana*)

pawpaw (*Asimina triloba*)

pokeweed (*Phytolacca americana*)

ramps (*Allium tricoccum*)

sassafras (*Sassafras albidum*)

staghorn sumac (*Rhus typhina*)

spicewood (spicebush) (*Lindera benzoin*)

sourwood (*Oxydendrum arboreum*)

black walnut (*Juglans nigra*)

wild mint (*Mentha* spp.)

wild strawberry (*Fragaria virginiana*)

# SOURCES

Bush, Florence Cope. *Dorie: Woman of the Mountains*. Knoxville: University of Tennessee Press, 1992.

Cooper, Nancy Blanche, ed. *Gatlinburg Recipe Collection*. Gatlinburg, TN: Crescent Color Printing Company, 1986.

Dabney, Joseph Earl. *Mountain Spirits: A Chronicle of Corn Whiskey from King James' Ulster Plantation to America's Appalachians and the Moonshine Life*. New York: Charles Scribner's Sons, 1974.

Dykeman, Wilma and Jim Stokely. *At Home in the Smokies*. Washington, D.C.: National Park Service, Handbook 125. 1984.

Egerton, John. *Southern Food: At Home, on the Road, in History*. Chapel Hill: University of North Carolina Press, 1987.

Farr, Sidney Saylor. *More Than Moonshine: Appalachian Recipes and Recollections*. Pittsburgh: University of Pittsburgh Press, 1983.

Fussell, Betty. *The Story of Corn*. New York: Alfred A. Knopf, 1992.

Hardeman, Nicholas. *Shucks, Shocks, and Hominy Blocks*. Baton Rouge: Louisiana State University Press, 1981.

Hertzberg, Ruth et al. *Putting Food By*. Brattleboro, VT: The Stephen Greene Press, 1973.

Kephart, Horace. *Our Southern Highlanders*. Knoxville: University of Tennessee Press, 1976. Reprint.

Moss, Kay and Kathryn Hoffman. *The Backcountry Housewife. Vol. I: A Study of Eighteenth Century Foods*. Gastonia, NC: Schiele Museum, 1985.

Oliver, Duane, comp. *Cooking on Hazel Creek*. Hazelwood, NC: 1990.

Page, Linda Garland and Eliot Wigginton, eds. *The Foxfire Book of Appalachian Cookery*. Chapel Hill: University of North Carolina Press, 1992.

Parris, John. *Mountain Cooking*. Asheville, NC: Asheville Citizen-Times, 1978.

*Sam Houston Schoolhouse Cookbook*. Maryville, TN: Sam Houston Schoolhouse Association, 1980.

Shelton, Ferne, ed. *Southern Appalachian Mountain Cookbook*. High Point, NC: Hutcraft. 1964.

Trout, Ed. *Historic Buildings of the Smokies*. Gatlinburg, TN: Great Smoky Mountains Association, 1995.

Ulmer, Mary and Samuel E. Beck, eds. *Cherokee Cooklore*. Published by Mary and Goingback Chiltoskey. Cherokee, NC: Museum of the Cherokee Indian, 1951.

White, Max E. *Contemporary Usage of Native Plant Foods by the Eastern Cherokees*, Appalachian Journal, Vol 2, No 4, Summer 1975.

Wigginton, Eliot, ed. *Foxfire 2, 3 and 4*. Garden City: Anchor Books, 1973, 1975, 1977.

Witthoft, John. *Cherokee Indian Use of Potherbs*, Journal of Cherokee Studies, Spring 1977.

# INDEX

Meats
& Main
Dishes

Cornbread & Biscuits

## ACKNOWLEDGMENTS

So many people helped in so many ways to make this cookbook possible, it is difficult to know where to begin acknowledging everyone properly. Beuna Winchester, Glenn Cardwell, Faye Cardwell, Louise Woodruff, Charles Woodruff, Bonnie Myers, Hubert Sullivan, Lucinda Ogle, Lois Caughron, Mary Chiltoskey, Duane Oliver, John Dunn, Earl Ramsey, John D. Webb, Karen Ballentine, and Elsie Burrell granted interviews and provided unique Smoky Mountain recipes. Without their generous assistance and response to unending questions, this book simply could not have happened. With characteristic mountain hospitality, these people opened their homes and their hearts to this project. Occasionally they opened their refrigerators and pantries too, and I was the lucky beneficiary.

Joan Green, archivist at the Museum of the Cherokee Indian in Cherokee, North Carolina, led me to helpful sources; the FFA of Bryson City (NC) High School, supplied a taste of real sorghum molasses and how it is made; John Coykendahl shared his knowledge of beans and other heirloom crops; Kitty Manscill and Wilma Dykeman gave leads and encouraging words.

Sidney Saylor Farr, and her publisher, graciously granted permission to reprint the following recipes: Moonshine, Ash Cake, Cracklin' Bread, Johnny-cakes, Pawpaw Bread, Old-Fashioned Souse, Pork Sausage, Backbones and Ribs, Fried Frog Legs, Apple Fritters, and Vinegar Pie from *More Than Moonshine: Appalachian Recipes and Recollections*, by Sidney Saylor Farr c 1983. Reprinted by permission of the University of Pittsburgh Press. Others who gave permission to reprint recipes include: Nancy Blanche Cooper, *Gatlinburg Recipe Collection*; Ruth S. Walker, Sam Houston Schoolhouse Association; Blanche McCarter, Crescent Printing Company, Gatlinburg; *Maryville Alcoa-Times*; Mary Chiltoskey, *Cherokee Cooklore*; and Duane Oliver, *Cooking on Hazel Creek*.

Special thanks to historian Tom Robbins of Great Smoky Mountains National Park, Glenn and Faye Cardwell, and Steve Kemp for reviewing and editing the manuscript, yeomen service.

Their comments were of inestimable value to the completeness and accuracy of the text. Any errors or omissions, though unintentional, belong to the author. Many thanks to Mary Ann Kressig, David M. Higgins, and Tom Robbins for creating the still life food photographs. Thanks also to Christina Watkins for her design talents and interest in this project and to John D. Webb and Florence Webb for use of their beautiful canned produce used in the cover photograph for this book.

Although words are inadequate, I extend deep gratitude to Annette Hartigan, John Hartigan, Steve Kemp, and Janet Rock, Smoky Mountain friends who have unfailingly given sustenance and support in so many ways for so many years. Finally, to my mom, Madeleine Houk, who nourished us well with her good, honest cooking; and to Michael, who helped taste-test the recipes and who made yet another journey with me.

## NOTES

# NOTES

## NOTES

# NOTES

## NOTES

# OTHER BOOKS ON THE SMOKIES

## THE WALKER SISTERS OF LITTLE GREENBRIER
by Rose Houk

Six women lived nearly their entire lives in a small log cabin deep in the heart of the Great Smoky Mountains. They grew crops, nurtured orchards, raised livestock; they spun their own wool, sewed their own clothing, made their own medicines, and in every way lived close to the bosom of the land. They were the Walker Sisters, famous for their earthy skills and genuine hospitality. When the national park was created, they could not bear to leave their mountain home, and finally were granted a lifetime lease and remained in the Great Smokies until 1964. Their home and farmstead is preserved in the park to this day and is visited by all those who choose to make the journey. 60 pages, filled with historic photos and modern images of the Walker Sisters Collection. #400730 $7.95

## THE CADES COVE STORY
by A. Randolph Shields

Randolph Shields, a scholar and former resident, relates the history of this beautiful, lively mountain community. Learn about farming, homelife, religion, and recreation in the cove. Delightful historic photographs. Softcover; 116 pages. #400055 $6.95

## THE CHEROKEES OF THE SMOKY MOUNTAINS
by Horace Kephart

This is the classic story by Horace Kephart of the Eastern Band of Cherokees and their tragic westward removal on the "Trail of Tears." Softcover; 48 pages. #400066 $4.95

## HISTORY HIKES OF THE SMOKIES Revised and Updated!
by Michal Strutin

For hikers who love history, this book is for you! It features in-depth narratives of the 20 most culturally-rich trails in the Smokies. Learn the stories behind the cabins, barns, chimneys, stone walls, machinery, and other features so often encountered on Smoky Mountain trails. Includes detailed trail maps, steepness profiles, and historic photos. 352 pages; handy pocket size. #400650 $12.95

Books are available at all park visitor centers or by contacting Great Smoky Mountains Association, 115 Park Headquarters Road, Gatlinburg, TN 37738. (865) 436-7318 or visit www.SmokiesInformation.org. All purchases benefit park!